# salmonpoetry

*Publishing Irish & International*
*Poetry Since 1981*

# Dante

# Paradiso

in a new version by

# David Rigsbee

Published in 2023 by
Salmon Poetry
Cliffs of Moher, County Clare, Ireland
Website: www.salmonpoetry.com
Email: info@salmonpoetry.com

ISBN 978-1-912561-43-8

Cover Image by *Catherine Carr Whittemore*
Cover Design & Typesetting: *Siobhán Hutson*

*Printed in Ireland by Sprint Print*

*Salmon Poetry gratefully acknowledges the support of
The Arts Council / An Chomhairle Ealaíon*

*To the Beloved*

# Acknowledgments

Many people have helped me along the way, and I would be remiss if I did not mention their names. At the top of my list is my daughter Makaiya Padron-Cruz, who came up with the idea in the first place. One day in New York City, where we were then living, I mentioned to her that I'd like to add another direction to the usual poem-essay-review round to which I seemed to be in perpetual (and centripetal) motion. She said, "Why not take on something amazing—like translating Dante?" I pointed out that Dante had been well served in English, but she immediately dissented, noting that that opinion really applied to the *Inferno*, but that few poets had tackled the pinnacle of the *Commedia*, the *Paradiso*. She pointed out too that I was drawn to impossible works and that surely the *Paradiso* qualified. "And what's more you'll be in heaven," she added. And so I have been, thanks to her.

Years ago, Dan Kinney of the University of Virginia was a multiplier of my interest in Western epic and Romance literature, and I am grateful for his instruction. Sarah V. Clere and Martha Regalis, two of my most knowledgeable and amiable co-teachers, helped me to frame the kinds of cultural questions that set the mind going in many directions, including heavenward. Both are polymaths of the classics and exemplary teachers, and I am fortunate to have taught with them. Besides the mention of W. S. Merwin in my endnote, other poets showed me examples of how the epic tradition, albeit often remote, strange, and corner-intuitive, continues to backlight the cultural spaces we presently occupy. I am thinking of Carolyn Kizer, Derek Walcott, David Slavitt, and Joseph Brodsky. I had many conversations through the years with Kizer, who, like Merwin, translated from a number of languages, and let me follow her lifelong dialogue with another eminent translator of poetry, Edmund Keeley. Kizer also led me to David Slavitt's translations of the classics, especially Ovid. I profited from his example. It was Brodsky, with whom I often spoke of Italy and the classics in the 1970s, who playfully suggested that, in profile, my nose bore some resemblance to Dante's. He once sent me a postcard whose inscription was, "If you want a rose, follow your nose." I have had many fruitful discussions with others about Dante, but I must mention the following, who in one way or another, helped me shape my thoughts, trim my prejudices, and otherwise inspire and encourage the undertaking: Jordan Smith, Adrian Frazier, Linda Gregg, Nickolas Pappas, Clair McPherson, Michael Hinds, Michael Waters, Peter O'Neill, Jill Bullitt, Robert McNamara, and Carolyne Wright. My wife, Liz, has given me encouragement and the grace of time away to think and work. I thank her for the love and patience such a project requires and for absolving me of my absences.

I also wish to acknowledge the following periodicals, in whose publications some of these cantos and the introduction previously appeared: *Connotations Press: An Online Artifact*, *The Cortland Review*, *The Galway Review*, *Live Encounters*, *A New Ulster*, *Nine Mile*, and *Poetry Northwest*.

# Contents

# Introduction

The *Paradiso* is the last of three canticles (books) that make up the *Commedia*, what has come to be known as the *Divine Comedy*. It is the conclusion to the pilgrimage undertaken by the character Dante (also known as the Pilgrim), and its subject is heaven, the realm of angels and souls of the deceased who have returned to God. The story of the *Commedia* takes place over Easter in 1300, and at the time of composition (ca. 1308–1320), Dante was in exile, having been banished by the Black Guelph faction of Florence while on a diplomatic mission to Rome. Although he expected to, he never returned to Florence. We hear the plaint in a famous passage from Canto XVII, where the soul of his great-great grandfather Cassiaguida prophecies:

> You shall abandon everything
> for which you care most deeply; this is
> the arrow that the bow of exile shoots first.
>
> You shall know how salty the bread
> of others is, and how hard a footpath
> takes you up and down another's stairs.

Like his revered Ovid, Dante was not one to wear his exile lightly, and we remain aware that for him this fact, the more it is processed, becomes metaphorical. It is surely a part of human nature to yearn for a sense of belonging, and in locating belonging's whereabouts, for any pilgrim to renegotiate a way forward. It is also a metaphor for humanity's fallen state: we begin in innocence and tumble into experience, to put it in Blakean terms. Finding the way back to a knowing innocence (if such were possible) does not prevent the Angel, installed by God, from keeping his post at the gate of Eden with a flaming sword. Just as his own exile informs the *Paradiso*, so too its direction moves away from that lamentable condition and bends toward belonging, which, in a theological and philosophical sense, equals unity with that which doesn't change, God. Indeed, the souls in the Inferno are there because they couldn't change, but the paradox that change must rise to the changeless, the realm of the Paradiso, is central to Dante's poem. The poem is nothing if not about the measure—in several senses—of its reach. Understanding that assertion will ramify as you note that Boccaccio added the word the "divine" to "comedy," and it stuck.

Not only is the *Paradiso* the final canticle, it is the least read. The reasons offered for this are various: some say it lacks the sensational imagery of the *Inferno* or the earth-grounded, edifying climb of the *Purgatorio*; others complain that it is abstract and doctrinal, easily falling into the esoteric discursive mode favored by the Church Fathers; still others hold that there is little to look at but whirling lights with faces inside, that it contains none of the drama found in the Ugolino and Paolo and Francesca episodes in the *Inferno* or the farewell to Virgil in the *Purgatorio*. These criticisms are not always unjust, but the fact is that, by the time our Pilgrim gets to Heaven, he finds himself in a realm beyond drama, a realm in which he is given the opportunity to return with a report of ineffable sights and sublime encounters. At the same time, it aims to transform, or at least ultimately to supplement, action with contemplation, desire with grace. The *Paradiso* is also more accountable to the mystery of its subject, the journey of love to Love, than the other two canticles, drawing upon and consolidating the most stringent resources of language to bring to account something that lies beyond language. He reminds us of the problems with his translation of this experience, reminding us what it is like to wake from a dream, then partially forgetting the details of the dream, and yet still to acknowledge the impact, which is undoubtable and profound. He does this through the entire warp and weft of the poem's fabric: imagery, metaphor, symmetry, the terza rima with its braided rhyme, all in the service of, and in homage to, a triune god, who goes by a number of names: the One, Love, the Holiest, God (and by implication, Jupiter). Yet he is adamant that we not diverge too widely from orthodoxy, the True Path, for divergence can lead to two errors: the belief that the plurality of belief is itself a good thing, and the substitution of clerical authority (i.e., Papal) for truth.

For Dante, the search for ultimate designs was not just the province of philosophers and theologians, but of every person seeking to square the desire for justice on earth with the love of God. In fact, the *Paradiso* shows Dante at full sail, not only describing what no one has experienced before— a tour of the universe in the company of his eidolon (Virgil), followed by his Beloved—but a face-to-face meeting with God, who has prepared a spectacular, cinematic reception worthy of Busby Berkeley. It is a full-scale dramatization, which is to say an embodied account (although strictly speaking, the only body is the Pilgrim's) of Dante's quest to bring ultimate questions and their answers in line with doctrinal positions that, for him, had the status of settled case law.

In spite of the greater popularity of the *Inferno* and the objections noted above, many have considered the *Paradiso* Dante's greatest work, approaching not only the face of God, but the limits of art. It raises the final, most exalted questions of which humans are capable: what is the good? How should we live? How do we resist error? What are our responsibilities to others? What are we allowed to know on our brief sojourn on earth? In addition to these questions, which get their sinew chiefly from Aquinas and Aristotle, it also raises the matter of the purpose of art and the reach of language. All of the poem is situated on a paradox: ultimate reality exceeds our means of describing it. Yet if our salvation depends on the formation of our will (Piccarda says in Canto III: "in His Will lies our peace"), how can we represent what is most important without falling into the error of concentrating on the part—our partial knowledge—at the expense of the whole? These may seem like academic questions unrelated to life as we live know it, but Dante was interested in the scope of human endeavor and in the question of how it was possible to unite with God, to go from fragmentary status to final wholeness. The *Paradiso* is his rejoinder to these questions.

We know what Eliot said, "Dante and Shakespeare divide the world between them. There is no third." He wasn't the only Modernist to approve of this medieval conservative Catholic: Yeats, Pound and Joyce were on board too. Dante continues to get lip service from survey courses, and his character's descent into the Inferno provides puissant metaphors for pop-psychological and mythical adventurers, as well as fodder for peddlers of wisdom literature. He is also a touchstone. To be a card-carrying Dantean is to be a connoisseur of the truly minute, as well as the sweeping. It is to follow the scrambled politics and loyalties of thirteenth century Florence, the personalities of popes and masters of the mace and sword, and the ideas by which they whet their blades. It is also to speak knowingly about Dante's predecessors, both epic—in particular Virgil, and recent— the Troubadours—and to be able to deliver a lecture on the *dolce stil nuovo*, the "sweet new style" of the sonnet and canzone. It's to know something of Ptolemaic astronomy, Aristotelian physics and ethics, and Neoplatonism, as well as the discourses of the Schoolmen. And of course it is to be conversant in Catholic lore, to know something of the theology of Aquinas and Augustine and the arguments of the Doctors of the Church, to say nothing of having the Bible by heart. It is to hold a custodial regard for Dante's poetics, particularly the celestial waltz that issues from his terza rima. For this sort of devotee, no translation will do.

But Dante's mythological, psychological, and ultimately spiritual account of an imaginary journey is, root and branch, itself a translation, both of deep spiritual events within the character(s), into a tale, and of the fashioning of these events into a coherent artistic experience via language alive to the beauty of its own conception and responsive to the curiosity of its reader. Moreover, Dante extends his exile from Florence into the realm of metaphor and general statement. We first see the Pilgrim who has lost his way, and we are made to understand that the confusion that attends being lost is widespread enough to require divine intervention, which, in the form of Virgil, also makes a poetic intervention. Thus, the correct path leads to salvation and to poetry of the highest order at the same time. In a sense, poetry is salvation, and to distinguish between the poet's work on paper and in his soul is to invoke a contrast at variance with what Heaney calls "the autonomous habits of the poet's mind." Much has been made of poetry's inability to deliver the very transport it sings about—and for good reason: poetry's means are historical (and hence mortal), while Heaven is the realm of the timeless. Poetry gives us the image of the timeless, without delivering on the implied promise of actual timelessness, and yet when idea and image are so closely bound at every point, you have to wonder why the difference makes a difference.

Dante is aware of the risk raised by his undertaking, and he puts his finger on it in the first Canto of the *Paradiso*: it's impossible. In the wonderful negative space that is poetry, what is ineffable is both palpably real and untranslatable. You must call it out in figures and tropes, all the while with the understanding that the product—the poem—is not telling it like it is. For this, Plato banished the poets, and yet here we are, nearly 700 years beyond Dante's terminus date, still reading descriptions, gauzy or bright, of the Beyond, and still reading translations, especially of Hell, which is more interesting to the peanut-crunching crowd that Plath imagined pressing in to see—in this case the animated horror vacui of tortured sinners. It doesn't take Shelley to remind us that poets are legislators too: they judge and lay down the law. Dante was himself as much a translator of laws into meaning as a poet, that is, as a maker. Like Milton after him, he wanted to justify the ways of God to men. That is but one of the things he wanted; another is answers. For Dante, God's is a closed system. And while dynamic, often whirling, or careening majestically on its divine course, it is philosophically closed, with God as the source of radiance, the unwobbling pivot, as well as the place where the buck stops. The buck in this case is the question of the nature of things. Most of us do not live in a closed system of this sort, and so Dante can strike us as more than a little inflexible and opaque, even cold, despite the merciful ministrations of his muse and Beloved, the famous Beatrice.

Our image of Dante, both the character and the poet, owes much to the introduction we make with him in Hell. By the *Purgatorio*, he is still the poetic and spiritual dependent of Virgil, and so both the initial and continued presence of that escort, the "master of earth's memory," underscores the fact that this journey, before it is anything else, is a poetic journey. By the time we reach the *Paradiso*, Virgil is left behind. Technically, he cannot ascend into heaven because the accident of his birth precedes the Christian era, but poetically speaking, he must leave Dante to make his own leap, this time in the company of the spirit of Beatrice. You might say he exchanges the poetic for the religious, and you would be right. But her expertise in directing Dante's tour is even more expertly evident than was the guidance of the author of the *Aeneid*. Hell was ordered, but it had the feeling of chaos. Heaven, by contrast, is ordered and orderly.

As Beatrice's psychotherapeutic powers disentangle, time and again, his confusions, Dante's understanding of God's love grows, and his understanding allows him to be drawn upward. Concurrently, he is remaking his poetry (and poetry itself), broadening it from a human medium to a divine one. The change from Virgil to Beatrice (and finally, to St. Bernard) figures a move away from the colorful delights of representational language to the shimmering harmonies and linked, chromatic dances of incandescence itself. Light is, as Yeats said of the soul, "self-delighting," even as it is under strict rank on rank (which, by the Victorian era, was in George Meredith's figure, not of love at all, but of "unalterable law"). We are closer to the Victorians than to Dante, and thanks to Meredith and earlier to John Milton, whose Satan was not the pelted, frozen monster of the *Inferno*, but the dissident striker of "Strict laws imposed, to celebrate his throne/ With warbled hymns," we understand why Satan's viewpoint matters. Many have felt this reading the *Inferno*. Until the somehow creaking, zomboid image of Satan arrives in Canto XXXIII, it is still possible to "understand" and so rationalize many of the of sins narrated by offenders.

Buck Mulligan in *Ulysses* said of Stephen Daedalus that Dante "drove his wits astray... with visions of Hell." Readers not steeped in the sump of Catholic theology may well question the degree of their engagement with poetry that presupposes superannuated beliefs and rather commit to a more detached appreciation, whether scholarly or aesthetic. This is especially so in poems where style and matter are so fused that it would take a curious reader indeed to insist on their separation. At bottom is the fundamental question of what reading requires, and in the case of a poem like the *Paradiso*, it becomes something like this: who is the better reader of a poem built on faith, a believer or a literary expert? A lover or a scientist with a lab coat and a clipboard? Eliot was of the opinion that the true appreciation must entail belief. Dante's first audience would have agreed: you can't separate the form from the content. But the spiritual carry-on for modern readers makes it less likely such a premise will be widespread. How then engage in secular appreciation of Dante's masterwork in belief's diminished condition? Romantics will argue that it is an act of imagination to imagine belief and therefore to feel the force of its logic. Old Believers, for their part, will argue that to have to contrive the imagination in this way is, all by itself, a failure of imagination. Is the *Commedia* an actual triumph of some sort, or a poetic triumph? Are the two collapsible? There are many holes down which readers may follow Dante's rabbit.

Ezra Pound, author of his own *Cantos*, declined to call the *Commedia* an epic poem. Policing of genres aside, three of the quartet of poets assigned by Dante to Limbo (Homer, Lucan, and Ovid) were epic poets, and his guide, Virgil, was considered the most comprehensive of epic bards; indeed by the Middle Ages, he had acquired the status of a magician. While his magic is no good in Paradise, his own epic, the *Aeneid*, was the foundational poem of Rome, and at length, of Christendom. Dante's ambition to join the company of poets in Limbo (accepted) is not just self-aggrandizement, it is a bid to advance the conditions of epic poetry as a genre of widest relevance. For example, Dante's Italian was meant as a demonstration that demotic language was capable of telling the story of God and love and should be acknowledged as such. The irony of course is that, as a poet who met the shades of the classical poets and sued for admittance, he didn't yet have the work to justify such a bid. The *Commedia*, when completed, would be that bid, and so Dante enjoyed a little postmodern moment, one that would have amused Borges, who points to a similar feat of legerdemain pulled off by Cervantes in *Don Quixote*.

Dante derived his physics from Aristotle, his cosmology from Ptolemy. The latter, in particular, helped create the geocentric world of the *Commedia*. That the earth is at the center should provide no solace for errant humans: Hell is located there too. Plus, earth is the end of the line. But just as the Love flowing from the Empyrean runs the engine of the universe, so there is an immense distance from earth to heaven. All the more remarkable, then, is Dante's tour through the nine concentric spheres that make up this cosmos. Dante is made more and more aware of speed as he ascends, just as he is made more and more aware of the increasing intensity of light. In Canto XXVI he briefly loses sight entirely, but when he regains it, he finds that he is seeing in a different way. The Ptolemaic model provided poets with a structural symmetry obsolete or, at the moldy least, esoteric since the Enlightenment, but it continued to spin off in metaphors long after the Copernican revolution. In Dante's case, the cosmological scheme enshrined the philosophy and the theology provided both an exemplary architectonics and explanatory power. His poetry followed suit with its own mania for symmetry, symbol, and allegoric possibility: consider only the numerology associated with the number three and its multiples. God wished to make Himself known through his creation, and at the same time to remain beyond. So it was the job of the Pilgrim (and in Dante's world we are all pilgrims), who was himself subject to the corruption of matter no less than to angelic beckoning, to exercise his will in such a way as to climb towards the source of love, namely God. He could do this by learning to read the creation in which he found himself. Dante's poem is thus one of education, and he frequently finds himself subject to tutelage, in the first two canticles from Virgil, and in the *Paradiso*, more intensely so, from

Beatrice. He also learns from the celestial worthies, both by hearing what makes dogma true and by interpreting (and prophesying) history. In both cases, Dante is careful to make plain his confusions. By the time Beatrice has assumed charge of his paideuma, she anticipates his vexations before he has had a chance to formulate them himself. The job of articulation and redescription take on a resonance in the *Paradiso*, especially. Hell is filled with a racket; the music of the spheres, meanwhile, is the harmony implicit in the logic of Love. The souls in the Empyrean, whose projections Dante meets as he makes his way, courtesy of the Beloved, upward through the spheres, can hear it, as can the Pilgrim. The question is, how do you describe a sound so that the memory of the sound comes through the image of the sound? The same goes equally, if not more so, for light.

As he tells us in *La Vita Nuova*, Dante met the 8-year-old Beatrice Portinari on May Day on the Ponte Santa Trinità in Florence. He claims to have set eyes on her only twice, the second time nine years later on the street, where she turned and greeted him. Dante records that he had a dream that night that led to the writing of *La Vita Nuova* and to the understanding that Beatrice had become his inspiration beyond courtly love conventions. She was to become his spiritual guide even as she remained his beloved. As a result, it is customary to see Beatrice as a girl and then as a woman, followed by Beatrice as a guiding spirit, so pure that she sits close to Mary in Heaven. That he conflates the two Beatrices should not surprise us. Beatrice married a banker before her death three years later in 1290, and Dante himself married Gemma Donati in1285 and fathered three children. And while Beatrice is clearly the ideal, she remains an historical woman. As late as Canto XXXI, a discerning reader can catch the wistful note of human desire, even though the pilgrim Dante is required to relinquish all claim to her in order to experience the vision of God to which she has so patiently and dutifully led him. St. Bernard remarks that "She urged me to leave my place and come to bring an end to your longing." Beatrice, for her part, is too wise not to know, as Dante more than once refers to her knowing smile and to her ability to read his thoughts. With Beatrice's departure in mind, I think it is helpful to look deeper into just this longing because if, in Eliot's phrase, human desire is "the intolerable shirt of flame which human power cannot remove," it must fall to a transhuman hand to remove it. Dante invents a word (*trasumanar*) early in the *Paradiso* to suggest that we must really give ourselves over to become ourselves (where "selves" no longer pertain) in the drawing up to God's love. While the Pilgrim says he felt as changed as Glaucus, whom Ovid tells us became like a god, he laments that the same cannot be said about words. Augustine makes a similar point. This explains the pilgrim Dante's sometimes quizzical wonder that souls he meets in the lower spheres are not smarting for the fact that they are not higher up. He learns that each is completely happy and within God's love according to his or her capacity. The question of capacity rounds us back to the question of language, of course. We can only know (or for that matter, express) according to our capacity, but our experience, in its fullness, is not to be fully accomplished in acts of "knowing."

The double nature of Beatrice should not come as a surprise to anyone acquainted with the tradition of courtly love, from which so many of our poetic conventions and tropes, even romantic love *tout court*, have evolved. One entailment of this ethos is that the lover could never finally have the beloved. Perhaps that *consummatum non est* is the point too, in the sense that incompleteness charges and recharges idealism.

Theologically, what results is a transfiguration: the Beloved is not only a person; she stands for that which draws the lover in the first place to the source of love. It is for this reason that Beatrice withdraws from Dante when he is ready to experience Love as unmediated wholeness. At this moment, he feels himself drawn into the process, so to speak, of Love's creative undertaking, which is to make unity manifest. A wholeness of unlimited magnitude is the chief characteristic of Heaven, and it is radiant, dispersing its energies all the way down into the sphere of mutability, whose chief characteristic is incompletion and discontinuous energy, though people possess a *sensus divinitatis* that, thanks to free will, can predispose us toward the unity that is God. The Resurrection provided the paradigm of that free will and established a new covenant whose completion put paid to the pilgrim's doubts and befuddlement. It also let the paradoxes on which poetry has placed its ancient pike, no longer in need of special pleading or the bending of aesthetics into a crutch, but as productive and dynamic. As the human object of desire, fully realized under Love's dispensation, Beatrice is not just the *idée fixe* of a massively complicated man and poet, held onto for dear life to pull the ship of orthodoxy into the channel. In fact, readers can't help but feel that she remains, through all her transformations, the object of desire up to and including the moment she diverts her smile. The poet seems to ask what the point would be of self-overcoming if he were to relinquish too the humanity of the human origin of love. Despite his towering art and encyclopedic hunger, his Michelangelo-esque ability to manage both the personnel and materiél with synoptic skill, he never gave up the Troubadour ethos, which is grounded in the human personal. Nor did he wish to. That was the poetic equivalent of his choice of Italian over the universal and approved Latin (the language of the Church) as making local language sovereign for the discourses of the mortal pilgrim and— which is very much to the point here—of God's celestial hosts.

Seamus Heaney writes that "he stands for the thoroughly hierarchical world of scholastic thought, an imagined standard against which the relativity and agnosticism of the present can be judged." This was the view of Modernist poets, Eliot and Pound especially, the latter of whom wrote his own epic, namely the *Cantos*, to judge the present through the lens of a mighty, if inscrutable, past. Mandelstam was the first of the Modernists to see Dante's project in terms of the joy of composition, where composition was less a matter of putting form to doctrine and more a matter of the relationship between sound and hearing, between mouth and ear. We have him to thank for reminding us that Dante's poem was rooted as much in nature as in the supernatural. It was the language "that we acquire without any rule, by imitating our nurses," as he puts it in *De Vulgari Eloquentia*. For a poet as obliquely removed as Robert Duncan, Dante represents "a world in speech." He speaks of the "sweetness" inhering in Dante's verse, harkening back to the "*dolce stil novo*," the legacy of Provençal and Sicilian troubadours, the sweetness leading to the lightness and the light.

If in Shakespeare love is ineffable, and the voicing of it either too understated or too overreaching, the disjointure opening the door to tragedy, Dante, by contrast, shows that love begins in the flesh but rises to the ineffable, a state in which the soul, shed of egotism and desire, finds Love and Will united. Dante first sees God as a reflection in Beatrice's eyes, and you can unpack that a good, long time. Heaven, the face of God, and his achievement in the poem are one and the same. Dante is not unaware of the audacity of suggesting that the completed poem and Heaven are, in some sense, the same achievement. The *Paradiso* is the canticle where we see Beatrice from beginning to, virtually, the end. Prior to her active guidance as they soar through the heavens she is a memory, a rumor, a spirit who delegates

Dante's guidance to others. But while Virgil guides Dante through hell and up the Mount of Purgatory, his authority derives more as from his status as master poet than it does from divine appointment. The poetic education he undergoes suffices to take him to the Garden at the peak of the Mount, but that is not enough to align his affections with each other: the journey to Paradise becomes an education and the consolidation of an orthodoxy surpassing any Papal doctrine. Which is not surprising, as the pilgrim's feet have left the ground, and will not touch terra firma again until the *Commedia* is over. Nor will the composition of the poem begin until the education is complete and the form dynamic, symmetrical, and self-regulating like the cosmos it takes as its subject; the result is a poem that is at once orrery, confession, and cathedral.

# Paradiso

# Canto I

[The invocation and overture. Beatrice introduces Dante to Heaven and briefly outlines its workings. Beatrice also makes Dante realize that, as a mortal, he has been transformed in order to experience the immortal.]

The glory of Him who moves all
fathoms the universe, radiating
in one part more, another less.

I was in the part of heaven that receives
most. Whoever descends from there                    5
can neither know nor say what he has seen

because approaching its desire
our intellect becomes so weighty
that the memory can't follow.

Still, as much of the holy kingdom                   10
as I could take away as treasure
will become the matter of my song.

Good Apollo, for this final labor
make me worthy of your courage
and the gift of your beloved laurel.                 15

Up to this time, one Parnassian peak
has been enough for me, but now
I need both to enter heaven's arena.

Enter my breast and blow as high
as you did when you pulled Marsyas'                   20
limbs out from their sheath.

O divine power, if you lend me
just the shadow of your image stamped
in my brain to manifest, you will find me

at the foot of your revered tree,                                    25
crowning myself with those green leaves
of which my theme and you make worthy.

So seldom do they gather, Father,
—it's the guilt, the shame of human bias—
to honor either poet or Caesar                                       30

that when someone desires leaves
from Peneian branches it should make
the Delphic God swell with happiness.

Great flame follows after a spark,
and it may be that another's superior song                           35
will elicit a response from Mt. Cirra.

The world's lamp rises to mortals
at different points, but where it joins
four circles with three crosses

it reaches a better course, moves                                    40
in conjunction with a higher star
and like this anneals and stamps

the mundane wax more in its own image.
The conjunction had made morning there,
evening here, and that hemisphere                                    45

was in light, this in darkness
when Beatrice turned to the left
and stood fixed toward the sun—

no eagle ever stared as straight.
And as a second ray will follow the first                            50
and reascend, pilgrim-like,

so her gaze entering my eyes
moved into my imagination, owned it, and I,
contra custom, stared into the sun.

There, more is permitted our powers    55
than is lawful here, being a place
made proper for the human species.

I did not bear it long, but neither
so briefly as to fail seeing its sparks
as molten iron from the fire;    60

and suddenly it seemed that day
was added to day, as if He Who Can
had hung another sun to adorn the sky.

Beatrice fixed her eyes
on the everlasting spheres; I turned
from the sun and fixed my eyes on her.    65

Watching her I was changed within,
as Glaucus changed, consuming  the herb
that made him the sea gods' companion.

Transcending the human cannot be    70
put into words: so let this stand as example
until God's grace makes it experience.

Whether it was the newest created part
that rose there is known only to you, Love,
Heaven's Governor, whose light lifted me.    75

When that wheel that spins by desire
for you captured my attention
with a harmony you temper and tune,

then it seemed to me the sun set fire
to so much of the sky that neither rain    80
nor river ever formed so wide a lake.

The sound's novelty and the great light
incited me to find out their cause: I was
more full of eagerness than I had ever been.

Then she who saw me as I saw myself,                    85
seeking to calm my baffled mind, started
speaking before I even had a question,

and she began, "You have weighed your
mind down with preconceptions; you can't
see what you otherwise could have.                      90

You are not on earth, as you seem to think;
but lightning, streaking from its site,
will not move as fast as you, returning home."

When I had been divested of the first doubt
by her brief words, she smiled, and I                   95
was nonetheless perplexed anew and said,

"Though satisfied at this great marvel
I have to wonder how my body rises
and transcends these lighter bodies."

At this, a sigh of pity, and then she                   100
directed her eyes to me with that look
that a mother gives to a babbling child,

and she began, "All created things
have an inherent order, and this is the form
in which the universe resembles God.                    105

Here, the higher creatures create
an imprint of eternal worth, which is the end
and which is made the law.

Within that order I speak of, all
natures are inclined, depending on station.             110
nearer or farther, to their source.

Thus these natures sail to anchorage
at different ports in the grand sea of being,
each according to its instinct.

This instinct bears fire to the moon:                    115
this is the instinct that moves the mortal heart;
this binds the earth and unifies it.

    Not only creatures innocent of reason
but also those who possess love and intellect
are struck by the arrow this bow shoots.                 120

    The Providence that governs
forever subdues with its light the heaven
wherein spins the most rapid sphere.

    Now we soar to that place, as if
to a predestined site, shot by that bow                  125
that always strikes its joyous target.

    It is true that, as form sometimes
fails to follow art's intention
because matter is deaf to the call,

    so this created being sometimes                      130
veers from the true course because he can,
and so goes astray, like lightning seen

    falling from a cloud, and man's
initial impulse, sidetracked
by false pleasure, turns him earthward.                  135

    You should be no more amazed
at your ascent, than at the rush
of a mountain freshet to the valley floor.

    If you, now free of impediment,                      140
had remained down below,
that would be a cause for wonder.

    At this, she returned her face to heaven.

# Notes

13. Good Apollo—The traditional invocation of the Muses is here addressed to the sun god, a surrogate for God.

16. one Parnassian peak—Parnassus has two peaks, one sacred to the Muses, one to Apollo (with perhaps a glancing reference to the Mount of Purgatory—his previous poem—also a "Parnassian" peak.

20. Marsyas—a satyr, who challenged Apollo to a contest to see whether the music of the flute he had found (discarded by Minerva) played a sweeter music than the god's cithara. The Muses were asked to judge, and losing, Marsyas was flayed alive by Apollo. Metamorphoses (VI, 383–91)

25. your revered tree—the laurel.

32. Peneian—of Thessaly. Peneus was a river god, the father of Daphne, whom Apollo pursued. The leaves are laurel (i.e. bay leaves).

37. Mt. Cirra—mountain sacred to Apollo.

50. no eagle ever stared as straight—It was medieval belief that an eagle could stare directly into the sun.

66. the everlasting spheres—Heaven is composed of nine concentric spheres (the sequential destinations of Dante and Beatrice), each here representing degrees of sanctity. Beyond the spheres lies the Empyrean, where God lives.

69. Glaucus—a fisherman, noticed that his catch revived when put on a special herb and leapt back into the sea. Glaucus consumed the herb himself and became a god.

79. a harmony—the "music of the spheres."

124. the most rapid sphere—the Primum Mobile, the outer sphere, which moves with the force of God's love.

# Canto II

[Dante introduces the metaphor of sailing: he is a sailor through the cosmos. Beatrice explains why there are spots on the moon, the nature of matter and of the spheres.]

O you who are in a little boat
eager to listen following behind
my ship that sails singing

turn back again to your shores
not out to sea since you could,                          5
in losing me, be lost yourselves.

I sail an uncrossed sea;
Minerva breathes, and Apollo pilots me,
while the nine Muses show me toward the Bears.

You other few who have turned                          10
your mouths in time to the angelic bread
on which human life is fed—hungering—here,

you may indeed launch your vessel
upon the sea, keeping within my wake
before the water levels out again.                          15

Those heroes who crossed over
to Colchis and saw Jason behind the plow
were not as amazed as you will be.

The perpetual, inborn thirst we feel
for the godlike realm bore us nearly                          20
as fast as the heavens you beheld.

Beatrice gazed upward, and I
gazed at her. In less time than it takes
an arrow to fly from the bow to its mark

I found myself borne to a place          25
where something wonderful drew me,
and she from whom I could not hide

my mind's need, turned to me
as joyful as her beauty, and said,
"Turn your mind to God in gratitude.          30

He has brought us to the first star."
We seemed in a cloud as brilliant, hard,
polished, and dense as a sunlit diamond.

The eternal pearl received us
the way water takes light rays into itself          35
and yet remains indivisible.

If I was body—and we cannot conceive
how things can share the same space,
as we do here, where body enters body—

then should our desire be even more          40
to see the essence in which we behold
how our natures' and God's unite.

There we shall witness as true
what we hold as faith here and not proven
but directly known like the first truth man believes.  45

I answered, "Lady, with the most devotion
possible, I thank Him who removed me
from the mortal world. But tell me,

what are the dusky spots on the body
of this moon that, down on earth, have led men          50
to spin the fabled story of Cain?"

She smiled momentarily, then said,
"Mortals can't unlock the truth
except with the key of the senses.

This should come as no surprise,                    55
when, pierced by amazement's arrows, you
realize that the senses give reason short wings.

But tell me what you yourself think.
And I: "What seems diverse on earth, is,
I think, caused by infrequent densities of matter.    60

And she: "If you listen carefully
to my rebuttal, you will come to see
that your beliefs are riddled with error.

The eighth sphere offers many lights
and you can make out that they, in size              65
and quality are stars with differing features.

If this were caused by rarity and density
alone, then all stars would share a single virtue
more or less or equally distributed.

Different virtues must be the fruits                 70
of diverse formal principles, but on your view,
if correct, just one would be left, the rest destroyed.

What's more, if rarity were behind
the dusky spots you mention, then this planet
would lack thoroughgoing matter                      75

or else, just as a body can alternate
fat and lean, so this planet would be,
like a book, presenting different pages.

To make a case for the first instance,
in an eclipse, the sun's light would have to show     80
through, as with translucent matter.

But this isn't the case. Therefore,
we should take up the latter instance—if I
refute that too then your opinion is surely false.

If the rare matter is not spread throughout                85
then there must be a limit, a point at which
the density doesn't allow the light through;

from this point the sun's rays
would be cast back, just as lead-backed glass
returns colored light in reflection.                       90

Now you might argue that where
a ray has been reflected from a more
remote place, it will show itself dimmer.

But were you to try an experiment,
you might be freed from your objection                     95
to find in it the fountainhead of your art.

Take three mirrors, place two
equidistant from you and a third between
but set farther back. Now turn

to face them and at your back                              100
have someone set a light so that it strikes
all three and all reflect the light to your sight.

Although the farthest image
is also of reduced size, you will observe
that its brightness is the same as the others.            105

Or, as the sun's warm rays touch
the snow, divesting it of its blankness
and cold—and your intelligence stripped

of error—I will leave you
with a luminescence so filled with living                  110
that the light itself trembles in your sight.

Inside the heaven of godly peace
a body revolves in whose might is contained
the being of whatever lies within.

The next sphere, myriad-eyed,                           115
confers being to the various essences within,
stars distinct, and yet all contained in it.

The other spheres, in their different ways,
deploy the distinctive powers they possess
in the cause of their own seminal workings.            120

These other spheres, as they go
from one stage to another, do so receiving
influence from above and then acting below.

Now pay attention to how I
make my way to reach the truth you seek;               125
that way you will learn to ford the stream.

The power and motion of the sacred spheres
derive their inspiration from the blessed movers
just as the hammer is roused by the smith.

And so the lighted heaven wheeling                      130
from the unfathomable Mind receives its stamp
and in that image it becomes the seal;

and as the soul within your dust
is shared by the different organs, each suited
to its individual labor, so does the Mind              135

in this way unfold its plenitude
which all the stars in turn multiply
even while revolving in its wholeness.

The various virtues are mixed
with each precious body that it quickens,               140
just as the life is blended with the soul.

From the happy nature of its source
the mingled virtue shines through the body,
just as the living pupil conveys the soul.

It is from this, not dense or rare                                    145
matter, that make the variations from light
to light; this is the formal principle, that produces

according to its virtue, dark and bright.


*Notes*

9. The Bears—the constellations Ursa Major and Ursa Minor.
17. Colchis and saw Jason plow—The King of Colchis offered Jason the
fleece if he would subdue two fire-breathing bulls, plow the field of Ares
with them and sow them with dragons' teeth, from which sprang warriors.
Dante's reference implies that he too intends to achieve the golden fleece.
31. the first star—i.e., the moon.
34. The eternal pearl—the moon.
64. The eighth sphere—the sphere of the fixed stars.
115. The next sphere—of the fixed stars.

# Canto III

[The sphere of the moon. Dante meets Piccarda, who explains why the unevenly placed souls in Heaven enjoy a perfect harmony.]

The sun which had previously warmed
my heart with love had now revealed,
by proof and reproof, truth's sweet face,

and I, confessing and convinced,
raised my head and brought my eyes                    5
to the level of hers to speak

but a vision appeared so close
that it gripped me, and my mind quite
forgot its confession and went blank.

As in transparent, polished glass                     10
or water still and undisturbed—
(but not so deep it blocks reflection)

the faint image of our face returns
to us so colorless our pupils might as well
be seeing a pearl on a white brow.                    15

I saw such faces eager to speak!
I made the opposite mistake of that man
who spied himself reflected in a pool.

As soon as I became aware of them
and thinking they were reflections, I turned          20
around to see who they were, and instead

I saw nothing. I turned my sight
forward into the light of my gentle guide
whose blessed eyes, as she smiled, glowed.

"Don't wonder if I smile," she said,                    25
"at your naive understanding. You don't yet
trust your steps to come down on the truth;

your mind tricks you into emptiness.
The forms you see are true substances
put here for falling short of their holy vows."          30

Therefore, speak with them, listen
and believe. For the true light that by itself
fulfills them does not let their steps wander."

So I turned to the shade who seemed
most eager to speak, and began                           35
as one bewildered by his own eagerness.

"O well-created spirit, who feels
in the rays of eternal life such a sweetness
that it cannot be known unless experienced,

it would gratify me so if you                            40
would tell me your name and fate." To which
she answered at once with smiling eyes:

"Our charity will never lock
the gate on a just desire any more than Love
would not want his court to be like Himself.             45

When I was alive in the world
I was a sister, a virgin, and if your mind will recall,
and my greater beauty now does not hide me,

you will recognize me as Piccarda,
posted here among the other blessed ones                 50
within the most ponderous of the spheres.

Our wishes, which only serve the flame
that is the pleasure of the Holy Ghost,
glory in being shaped to His order.

And we are to be found                                    55
within so seemingly low a sphere
because our vows fell short of fulfillment."

    And I to her: "There is something
wonderful in your face that glows divinely
transmuting the look you once had.                        60

    Thus I was slow to recognize you
but with what you have told me now
I can make out your features more readily.

    Yet I wonder, you who are happy,
do you want to rise to a higher place                     65
in order to discern more and to be nearer Him?"

    She smiled a little with the other shades
but promptly answered me with such rapture
it was as if she shone with love's first fire.

    "Brother, the power of heavenly virtue                70
quiets the will, and we are desirous for what
we have, not thirsting for what we do not.

    If we longed for what was higher
our desire would be discordant with the wish
of Him who wills us to this sphere.                       75

    Such discord you'll not find here
for to exist in love here is our necessity,
if you think about the nature of love.

    Indeed, the essential blessedness
of this state is to be at one with the Divine             80
Will that wills our own wills to His.

    So that our postings from rank
to rank please this realm, as they please
the King whose Will it is to will us.

And in His Will lies our peace—                    85
it is a sea where all beings are drawn, a sea
He creates and nature carries forward."

Then it became clear to me how
everywhere in heaven is Paradise, where yet
supreme grace need not rain down uniformly.      90

But as it chances that sometimes
one is sated by some food, yet craves another,
giving thanks for this thing, yet asking for that,

just so I pleaded with her by word
and sign to say what cloth she had failed          95
to draw through the shuttle, her unfinished vow.

"A perfect life and celestial merit
preserve a higher lady," she said, "in whose rule
some on earth assume the tunic and veil

and who until death both keep watch            100
and sleep, receiving the Bridegroom for whom
all love's vows conform to His pleasure.

As a young girl I left the world
to keep to her and enclosed myself in a habit,
promising to follow the path of her order.        105

Then men more used to hatred
than love came and tore me from the cloister:
God knows what my life became then.

This other bright figure you see here
to my right, who reveals herself to you, kindled   110
with all the luminescence of our sphere,

well understands my words: she too
was a sister and from her head, as with mine,
they tore the shadow of the holy veil.

But though she was returned 115
by force to the world, and against her honor,
she never let go the veil covering her heart.

This was the glory of the great Costanza
who, married to Swabia's second gust of wind,
gave birth to a third and final rush of power." 120

Having said this, she began to sing
"Ave, Maria" and while singing she sank
and faded like a weight vanishing in water.

I followed her as long as I could
until she disappeared, and then I turned 125
my sight to the greater object of my longing

which was Beatrice,
but so forceful was the light from her
that struck my eyes, it at first it blinded me

and I was slow to resume my questioning. 130

*Notes*

15. a pearl on a white brow—Like Milton's "darkness visible," the paradox of
this image typifies Dante's project: to render what is impossible.
17. that man—i.e., mistaking real persons for reflections. The reference is to
Narcissus.
49. Piccarda—Piccarda Donati. Piccarda was the sister of Dante's friend
Forese (*Purgatorio* XXIII, 48) and of the warrior Corso (*Purgatorio* XXIV, 82
ff). Dante was himself married to Gemma Donati. Piccarda was forced by her
brother Corso to marry a Florentine. Sickened at having to abjure her vows,
she died soon afterward.
97. A higher lady—Clara of Assisi, a disciple of St. Francis and founder of an
order.
122. Costanza—The Empress Constance (1154–1198). As Empress of the
Two Sicilies, she married Emperor Henry VI and became mother of Frederick
II. Legend has it that she was a nun who was forced to marry Henry.

# Canto IV

[Piccarda instructs Dante in free will and declares Plato's doctrine of the
origin and return of souls incorrect.]

Equidistant between two morsels of food,
though he were free to choose, a man would fail
to set his teeth in either and rather die of hunger.

So would a lamb stand paralyzed
between starved wolves, fearing both,                    5
so would a dog transfixed between two deer.

Likewise if I stood there speechless,
I would neither praise nor blame myself, so pulled
would I be by the necessity of my doubts.

I held my peace, but the longing                         10
and questioning written on my face, spoke
far more eloquently than any speech.

Then Beatrice did as did Daniel
when he lifted Nebuchadnezzar from the rage
that made him so unjustly cruel.                         15

She said, "I can see how your desires
pull you two ways at once, so that your fervor
ties itself up and leaves you choked for words.

You argue this way: 'If my good will
endures, how can the violence of others                  20
diminish the full measure of my reward?'

A second thought gives you occasion
for doubt: that after death all these souls
seem to return to their stars, just as Plato said.

These questions bear equal weight                    25
in vying for your will. So I will treat first
the one whose poison is more deadly.

Neither the most godlike Seraphim,
not Moses, Samuel nor whichever John
you prefer, I say, not even Mary herself          30

have their seats in any other heaven
than that of these spirits you have seen
here, nor has age to do with what is eternal.

But all beautify the primal sphere
differently and enjoy sweet life there, varying      35
only in how they feel the eternal breath.

These souls revealed themselves, not
because it is their allotted sphere, but as a sign
that here the celestial favor is least exalted.

I speak using such signs                              40
because your mind must first make out
by the senses what it then renders intellectually.

It is for this reason that Scripture
condescends to attribute hands and feet
to God, while meaning something else              45

and the Holy Church gives
Gabriel and Michael human features
and that other who restored Tobit's sight.

If one took literally what *Timaeus*
says about the soul it would be completely          50
unlike what one sees to be the case here:

he says that the soul returns to
the star from which it took leave in order
to frame in Nature its particular substance.

It may be that his doctrine is disguised          55
so that the words sound, and may indeed
possess, a meaning not to be derided.

If he means that these wheels return
the honor and blame that results from their
influence, then his arrow may have hit the truth.          60

This principle, misunderstood, warped
nearly the world into bestowing such nomenclature
as Jupiter, Mercury, and Mars on the planets.

The other doubt that troubles you
has less venom for its malevolence is not such          65
that it could make you stray from my side.

In the eyes of mortals our justice
can been seen as injustice, which is by itself
a mark of faith, not heretical wickedness.

But since your intellect can penetrate          70
this truth and understand it without difficulty
I will, as you desire, explain it to you.

If, when violence occurs, the victim
contributes nothing to the violent act,
he cannot be exonerated on that account;          75

for will, if it will not, never abates
but acts as a flame does in nature, though
brute force try to snuff it a thousand times.

So that will assists force regardless,
whether it yields much or little, as these souls did          80
who could have retreated to their cloister.

If their will had been as intact
as that which held Lawrence to his grill
and made Mucius offer up his own hand,

then as soon as they were free they                    85
would have found the true path from which
they had been dragged—but seldom is it so.

    And by these words, if you fathom
them aright, you see how they have closed a case
that would have bedeviled you incessantly.          90

    But now another pass that must be
crossed bars your view; you would never
make it through on your own, so exhausting is it.

    I have made you believe for certain
that these blessed can never lie because            95
they are always near the First Truth;

    then you heard Piccarda say
that Costanza had never dishonored the veil,
and here Piccarda seems to contradict me.

    Often, my brother, it has happened             100
that men, in order to escape greater danger,
choose to do what they never would have done;

    so Alcmeon, incited by his father's prayer,
cruelly killed his mother, rather than face the sacrilege
of not having acted in accordance with piety.       105

    At this point I would insist you remember
that force and will can combine to cause
offenses that no excuse can ever justify.

    Absolute Will does not yield to wrong
but may consent conditionally if it fears a worse   110
trouble will result from its resistance.

    Therefore when Piccarda spoke it was
the Absolute Will she meant, and I meant
the other. Both of us have spoken the truth."

Such was the flowing of the holy river              115
which issued from the Fountain of All Truth
that it put both of my doubts to rest.

"Beloved of the First Love, Divine Lady,"
I said then, "you whose words inundate and warm
me so that I am more and more revived,              120

there is not enough depth in all my love
to offer sufficient grace for your grace, but may
He who sees and can, be my response.

I do recognize that our intellect is never
satisfied unless it bears Truth's illumination,     125
beyond which nothing true can come into being.

Once the mind of man has reached
inside that Truth, like an animal secure in its den,
he has attained his desire—if this is not so, then

all is vanity! So the foot of truth finds            130
also doubt's tendrils; that is the thing that drives
us from height to height, toward a summit.

I am encouraged, Lady, just as I am
heartened and inspired, to ask you, in reverence,
about a truth that is still obscure to me.           135

I wonder if in your view someone can make
amends for vow-breaking through good works
and not be found wanting in the balance."

Beatrice looked at me with eyes sparkling,
so full of divine love that the strength of my own   140
sight was easily overpowered, and I cast

my eyes down, close to fainting.

## Notes

13–14. Daniel when he lifted Nebuchadnezzar—King of Babylon, condemned his counselors to death when they were unable to interpret a troubling dream. Daniel, however, divined the dream and its interpretation (Daniel 2:1–46). Beatrice, by analogy, knew both Dante's concerns and their solution.

22. A second thought—This thought is discussed in *Purgatorio* XVI, 58–81, as erroneous because it would deny free will.

48. that other who restored Tobit's sight—Raphael, the archangel.

49. *Timaeus*—Plato says, in the *Timaeus*, "He who lived well during his appointed time was to return to the start which was his habitation, and there he would have a blessed and suitable existence." (Jowett translation [41, 42]).

61. This principle—i.e., that souls return to the stars from which they issued.

83. Lawrence—St. Lawrence, the deacon of Rome, was martyred for offering up the poor to the Prefect as the one treasure of the Church. Roasted on a grill, he is reported to have said to his torturer, "You have roasted one side, tyrant; now turn the other and eat."

84. Mucius—A Roman who vowed to assassinate the Etruscan king Porsena, mistakenly attacked a similarly attired secretary and was captured. Mucius boasted to the King that he was but the first of 300 who would launch similar attacks and to prove his valor, he thrust his hand in the fire, earning him his freedom and, according to Roman historian Livy, a peace treaty.

103. Alcmeon—Forced to kill his mother on the command of his father, as related by Euripides, recounted by Aquinas and discussed by Aristotle in the *Nicomachean Ethics* (Book III).

# Canto V

[Beatrice explains free will and the nature of vows. They ascend to the second sphere, that of Mercury, where they meet the Emperor Justinian.]

"If in love's warmth my flame swells
with a radiance never seen on earth
beyond vision's capacity to perceive

don't marvel; it comes from perfected
vision that sees the good, and the more          5
it sees, the more it is drawn there.

Already I see that your intellect
shines with Eternal Light, which, once
seen, forever shines and ignites love.

And should some other thing seduce          10
your love, it's only a misunderstood vestige
of the greater light that shines through it.

You want to know if is possible
by a righteous act to repair a broken vow
and so secure the soul against litigation."          15

Thus Beatrice began this canto,
and being one who would not interrupt
her speech, so her holy undertaking continued.

"The greatest gift that God in his largesse,
in the midst of creating, gave, that gift most          20
matching his goodness, that He Himself

holds at the highest worth—is free will.
Creatures with intellect, and only they
were and are so exclusively endowed.

Just so it will be seen in how                            25
high esteem this vow is held when God
joins with you in mutual consent;

this is because when man's and God's
purposes are compact, man sacrifices
this treasure, this free will, to the will of God.        30

What compensation can there be?
To reuse the already offered would be the same
as something ill-gotten used to do good work.

By now you understand the main point,
but since the Holy Church assigns dispensations,          35
which seems contrary to the truth I've shown you,

it behooves you to keep your seat
a little longer at table because the heavy food
you have consumed takes longer to digest.

Open your mind to what I will show you                    40
and keep it close within, for it is pointless to hear
a thing, if what is heard is not retained.

Two things are essential when one
makes a sacrifice: one is the thing itself;
the other, the compact to which one consents.             45

The latter cannot be cancelled until
the compact is carried out; this is what
I explained to you so precisely earlier.

Thus making sacrifice was required
of the Jews, but as you know, they could alter           50
their offerings by introducing substitutes.

The other vow, the so-called matter,
may well be such that it does not put one
at fault if it is made to substitute for another.

But let no man alter that burden                    55
on his own judgment without waiting
for the gold and silver keys to turn first;

and let him see that any change
is pointless unless the thing put by contains
the alteration, as six contains four.                60

But there are some things that,
once a vow is made, take on such weight
that for them there can be no substitution.

One should never make a vow rashly.
Be constant. Do not utter an impulsive oath          65
as Jephthah did when he made his sacrifice.

Better to have said, "I erred,"
than exceed the mistake in keeping the vow.
Think of the Greeks' great commander whose

Iphigenia wept for her beauty and made              70
wise and foolish cry alike when they heard
the wretched account of that dreadful rite.

Christians, move slowly, seriously.
Don't be a wind-puffed feather; neither presume
that every wash you take is a baptism.               75

You have both Testaments, Old and New
and you have the Shepherd as constant guide;
this much will suffice for your salvation.

If evil greed tempts you astray,
be men, not silly sheep, to whom the Jew             80
resident among you may snicker in derision.

Do not be like the foolish lamb that bolts
from its mother, only to accost itself in fighting
and has nothing but self-harm as its result."

Thus Beatrice to me, even as I have                        85
written. Then full of longing, she turned herself
toward that part where the world is more alive.

She was silent and her aspect changed,
forcing me to quell my thoughts, when my mind
was now ready to take on new questions.                    90

And just as an arrow pierces its mark
before the bowstring has even come to rest
so did we shoot up into the second realm.

I beheld my Lady so delighted there
when she crossed over into that heaven                     95
that the planet grew brighter from her joy.

And if the planet itself smiled, what
then of me, who by nature am made
for mutability, subject to every change?

Just as in a pure and tranquil pool                        100
fish are drawn to the surface by the hint
of some edible morsel fallen in, so I saw

more than a thousand splendors
moving our way, and each one intoned,
"Here is another to increase our love."                    105

And as each one approached, such
was the joy that I could discern the soul
within glowing with its own incandescence.

Think about it, reader, imagine
if I stopped my story now and wouldn't                     110
continue, how you would beg me to relent

and you will understand how intent
I was to hear the stories of these souls
the instant they appeared before my eyes.

"O well-born soul, to whom it is                    115
given to see the thrones of eternal triumph
before the warfare of life is deserted,

the light that shines through all
of heaven is in us, so if you desire, ask
until your appetite to know is satisfied."          120

Thus spoke one of the spirits,
and Beatrice followed: "Speak fearlessly,
and believe them as if they were gods!"

"I can see how you have nested
in your own light and how the rays behind          125
your eyes shoot out when you smile.

But I do not know who you are,
nor why you are stationed in this sphere
where another planet's rays conceal your rank."

I said this to the light that first                 130
had spoken to me; and at this it burned
more brilliantly than it had before.

Just as the sun, when its cumulative
force has broken through thick fog, is itself
concealed in the extravagance of its light,         135

by greater rapture thus concealed
itself in its own radiance, a saintly figure
so closed and so enfolded, answered me

in the way that the following canto sings.

## Notes

66. Jephthah—King of Israel. After victory over the Ammonites, he promised to offer up to God the first thing that came out of his door. His daughter emerged, and he killed her.

69. the Greeks' great commander—Agammemnon, who sacrificed his daughter Iphigenia in order to appease Artemis, whom he had offended. She responded by calming the sea. With Iphigenia's death, the ships were then able to set sail for Troy.

95. she crossed over into that heaven—The second sphere, that of Mercury.

121. one of the spirits—The Emperor Justinian (482–56 A.D.)

# Canto VI

[Justinian relates the story of his conversion from heresy and the codification of laws. He then narrates the history of the Roman kingdom and its transformation to the Republic, the Empire, and the Holy Roman Empire.]

After Constantine turned the eagle
counter to heaven's course, its flight followed
behind the ancient who had married Lavinia;

century after century and more,
God's raptor remained shut off at Europe's                    5
farthest edge, by peaks from which it emerged;

beneath the shadow of blessed wings
it ruled the world, moving from hand to hand
until, so changing, it reached my own:

I was Caesar and am Justinian                                  10
who, by the will of Primal Love I feel, removed
what was extreme and useless from our laws.

Before I began my work I thought
that Christ possessed but one nature,
no more, and I felt satisfied in this belief,                 15

but blessed Agapetus, he who
was highest shepherd, pointed me
toward genuine faith with his words;

I did believe him, and now clearly see
what his faith was, as truly as you can see                   20
how contradictions are at once true and false.

As soon as I walked in step with
the Church, God in his grace inspired me
to service for which I brought myself whole.

To my Belisarius I gave arms,                    25
for God's right hand favored him: it was
a sign for me to rest from warfare.

This is my answer to your first
question, and yet the answer is such
that I must add to it, to make clear          30

how empty it is when they attack
the sacred standard, whether they be those
who affirm or those who oppose it.

See what virtue made it worthy
of reverence, beginning from the time Pallas     35
gave his life to endow it with sovereignty.

Well you know that for three hundred
years and more it stayed in Alba, until
at last three against three fought for it.

You know what transpired through          40
seven kings, from the Sabines' to Lucretia's rape,
and how it grew by plunder of neighboring lands.

And you know what it did when carried
by brave Romans against Brennus and Pyrrhus,
and other principalities and areas.          45

Thus Torquatus and Quintius, so named
for his curly locks, the Decii and Fabii achieved
a fame it is my pleasure to honor.

It knocked down the Arabian pride
that trailed after Hannibal when he crossed          50
the Alps from which you, Po, glide down.

Underneath that standard, young Scipio
and Pompey triumphed, and it showed its fury
against the hill at whose bottom you were born.

Then, when the time came, heaven                    55
willed that the world resemble it in serenity;
Caesar bore the standard, by the will of Rome.

What then happened: it viewed Isère,
Loire, and Seine from Var to Rhine and all valleys
whose freshets cascade to fill the Rhone.          60

What then happened: it was such
flight from Ravenna to Rubicon that no tongue
could ever proclaim, nor pen describe, in words.

It wheeled its legions into Spain,
then to Dyrrachium, and then hit Pharsalia        65
so hard that even the hot Nile felt pain.

It saw its source again: Simeois
and Antandros, and Hector's grave; then roused
itself to flight once more—the worse for Ptolemy.

Swift as lightning, it fell on Juba                70
then it turned around again to strike your west
where Pompey's bugle could be heard.

Because of what that standard did
with its next bearer, Cassius and Brutus howl
in the inferno, and Modena and Perugia cry.       75

Wretched Cleopatra still weeps, who,
fleeing before the standard, finally met
black and sudden death from a viper.

With him it stretched to the Red Sea,
with him it brought a universal peace             80
that kept Janus' temple doors bolted.

But what this standard, that bears
my theme, had done before and would do
yet to the mortal realm that lay beneath,

and all of this appear in shadow,                                    85
unless we see with clear eye and true heart
as it appears in the Third Caesar's hand.

For the living justice that moves me
allowed it, in the hand I speak of, the glory
of vengeance for His displeasure's sake.                             90

Now be awed by what I tell you:
afterwards with it raced with Titus to avenge
the vengeance taken for the ancient wrong.

Now when Lombard tooth bit down
on Mother Church, victorious Charlemagne,                             95
under those wings, came to rescue it.

Now you have the power to judge those
whom I previously accused, and judge their crimes,
which are the cause of all of your offenses.

One side sets yellow lilies against                                  100
the public standard; the other appropriates it
for its own: it's hard to tell which sins more.

Let them hatch their plots, the Ghibellines,
under some other banner, for those who wrongly
follow this sign, severing justice, are henchmen.                    105

Nor let the new Charles bring it down,
he and his Guelphs, but let him feel claws
that have ripped flesh from fiercer lions.

So often children weep for their
fathers' sins; let him not imagine his *fleur-de-lis*               110
will supplant the crest on God's coat of arms.

This little star will accompany those
good spirits who have been active in order
that fame and honor might succeed them:

And when desires bend toward earthly                    115
things, deviating, then true love drives its rays
upward with lesser intensity toward heaven.

Our joy is partly to observe the balance
between merit and reward because we see
them as equivalent, neither greater nor less.          120

Therefore living justice affects us so
sweetly that we are made free, no longer
liable to be twisted toward any iniquity.

Just as diverse voices in our lives
make sweet tones, so different ranks compose           125
sweet harmony among these spheres.

Within this pearl there shines
a radiance like that of Romeo, whose deeds,
though beautiful and bold, went ill-rewarded.

The Provençals who schemed against                     130
him will not have the last laugh: whoever
resents another's good travels an ill way.

Raymond Berenger had four daughters
and each a queen, owing to the efforts
of Romeo, a humble man and a pilgrim.                  135

But envious words so moved Raymond
that he demanded this just soul make an accounting,
this man who had made him twelve for ten.

Romeo left old, stooped and poor.
And if the world could know his heart, as he           140
trudged begging door-to-door, then as much

praise as now he has, he would have more.

# Notes

1. the eagle—The standard of Empire, and, later, symbol of God's empire. After Constantine turned the eagle "counter to heaven's course" (west to east) by moving the seat of power from Rome to Constantinople, he also, by Dante's lights, countered God's will that the seat of power remain in Rome. Constantine believed this was his gift to the Church (the "Donation of Constantine").

2. Lavinia—The second wife of Aeneas. The marriage symbolically linked the Trojan culture to what would later become the Roman. Aeneas was considered the founder of what would become the Roman Empire. Lavinia was Etruscan.

10. I was Caesar and am Justinian—Justinian became Roman Emperor in 527. After his conversion, he turned to codifying Roman law.

16. Agapetus—Pope 535–536.

25. Belisarius—Justinian turned military affairs over to his general, Belisarius.

35. Pallas—In the *Aeneid*, Pallas establishes a kingdom on the site of present-day Rome, which Aeneus acquired after Pallas was killed by Turnus in battle.

41. from the Sabines' to Lucretia's rape—In Roman mythology, the early Romans abducted women from outer regions in order to establish new families. According to the Roman historian Livy, Lucretia was a Roman woman whose rape by the last of the tyrannical Roman kings led to the establishment of the Roman Republic.

44. Brennus and Pyrrhus—Gallic chieftain and Kind of Epirus, in Greece: enemies of Republican Rome.

46. Torquatus and Quintius—The Republican Torquatus defeated the Gauls. Quintius, also known as Cincinnatus, famously left his plow to become dictator of Rome.

47. Decii and Fabii—Roman families renowned for their adherence to martial duty. It was one of the Fabii, Quintus, Maximus Maximus, who defeated Hannibal during the Gallic Wars.

50. Hannibal—Carthaginian commander during the second Punic War (264–241 BC).

52. young Scipio—Scipio Africanus defeated Hannibal in Spain in 221, when he was twenty. He invaded Africa at thirty-three and brought about the fall of Carthage (and Hannibal). Pompey's first victory came when he was twenty-five.

65. Dyrrachium—Site of the interim victory (48 BC) of Pompey over Caesar.

65. Pharsalia—Site of the subsequent and decisive victory of Caesar over Pompey (as related by the epic Roman poet Lucan, who appears with Homer, Ovid, and Horace in Limbo, in *Inferno*, IV).

67. Simeois, the river in Asia Minor, near Antandros, from which Aeneus set out for Italy.

68. Hector's grave—Hector was Trojan champion and prince, defeated in battle by Achilles.

69. the worse for Ptolemy—Because, moving to Egypt, Caesar defeated Ptolemy.

70. Juba—King of Numidia (56 BC). He was defeated by Caesar.

74. Cassius and Brutus—Assassins of Julius Caesar.

75. Modena and Perugia—In 41 BC Augustus, Caesar's nephew and future emperor, defeated Mark Antony's brother at Perugia. He defeated Mark Antony at Modena in 43 BC.

76. Cleopatra—the last active pharoah of Egypt. After her death, Egypt fell under the rule of Rome.

81. Janus' temple doors bolted—The gates to the Temple of Janus were kept open in time of war.

87. the Third Caesar—Tiberius. The Crucifixion occurred under his reign.

92. Titus—The emperor Titus (39–81 AD), defeated the Jews in Jerusalem (70 AD), hoping, by annihilating the religion, to take "vengeance…for the ancient wrong."

94–95. Lombard tooth bit down on Mother Church—Desiderius, King of the Lombards, rebelled against the Church but was defeated by Holy Roman Emperor Charlemagne in 774 AD.

95. Charlemagne—(742–815). The King of the Franks united much of Europe in the Middle Ages and became the first Holy Roman Emperor, claiming succession to the collapsed Roman Empire of antiquity.

100. yellow lilies—i.e., France.

101. the public standard—i.e., the Eagle.

101. the other—The Ghibellines.

106. the new Charles—Charles II of Anjou (1254–1309) led the Guelphs.

111. the crest—i.e., the Eagle.

128. Romeo—Romeo da Villanova (1170–1250), a successful prime minister of Raymond Berenger IV, Count of Provence, who, falsely accused of mismanaging the treasury, picked up his pilgrim's staff and left the court. Among his successes had been the negotiation of each of Berenger's four daughters to a king.

133. Raymond Berenger—Count of Provence (1209–1245).

# Canto VII

[Beatrice explains how vengeance can be just, why God chose to redeem mankind through the Crucifixion, and how God's magnanimous nature, in sacrificing His Son, is a greater act than the pardoning of sins.]

*"Osanna, sanctus Deus sabaòth,*
*superillustrans claritate tua*
*felices ignes horum malacòth."*

Thus, as he whirled to his own music
I saw that substance sing, above                    5
which a doubled light itself doubled

and the others moved to their dance
and then like a spray of sparks they faded
and disappeared in the distance.

I hesitated and he said, "Speak!                    10
Speak!" And to myself: "Speak to her
who quenches thirst with her sweet drops."

But the wonder that overtakes me
at the sound of BEA or ICE made me
bow my head like one fallen asleep.                 15

But Beatrice ended that, as she
smiled with such radiance that even
a man set aflame would rejoice.

"According to my unfailing sense,
you don't yet understand how just                   20
vengeance can be avenged justly.

But I will quickly settle your doubts,
so pay heed: what I have to tell you
will bestow a gift of highest truth.

Because he wouldn't suffer a power                25
that would curb his will, the unborn man,
in damning himself, damned his progeny.

As a result, the human species
lay sick for centuries, sunk in error, until
it pleased the Word of God to descend             30

to the point at which its estranged
nature was rejoined to Him in person
with the sole act of His eternal love.

Now, listen closely to my reasoning:
joined again to its first cause, this nature      35
as when created, was good and just

but by itself alone was expelled
from paradise because it veered
from the way and the life of truth.

If the penalty the cross exacted                  40
is measured by the nature it assumed,
none has ever been stung with such justice.

And none ever suffered so great injustice,
considering the person who endured it,
with whom the other nature was fused.             45

Therefore, from one act, diverse things,
a single death pleasing to God and to the Jews,
for which earth trembled and heaven cracked.

It should no more seem hard to grasp,
when it is said that just vengeance               50
was afterward by a just court avenged.

But now I see your mind is tangled,
ties thought on thought into a knot
from which, waiting, it hungers for relief.

You say, 'I understand what you                    55
are saying, except for this: why God willed
this as the only way for our redemption.'

This decree, brother, is kept from
the inner eyes of all who have not yet
grown to fullness in the flame of love.             60

Nonetheless, though one gazes
long at the mark—with scant discernment—
I will tell you why this way was fitting.

Divine Goodness, that rejects
all envy in itself, so sparkles in its burning       65
that it reveals eternal grace.

Everything that derives from this
Good is boundless because His seal,
once imprinted, can never be erased.

Whatever then pours forth                           70
is unimpeded because it is not subject
to the influence of lesser things.

The more it conforms, the better
it pleases; the Sacred Ardor shining in all
things glows most near those things like itself.    75

The human has the advantages
of these things, and if he fails in one,
he necessarily plummets from his nobility.

Only sin undoes man's freedom
and makes him unlike the Highest Good                80
so that Its light, within his human glow, dims,

and his dignity will never return
if he doesn't fill transgression's void
with suitable amends for illicit pleasure.

When your nature at the root so                    85
grossly sinned, it was exiled from this honor
just as it was expelled from Paradise.

Nor could man recover what was lost,
if you mind my words subtly, by any other way,
except by crossing one of two fords:                90

either God alone pardoned
through His mercy, or man himself had
to offer suitable recompense for his folly.

Now fix your eye down into the deep
of the Eternal Counsel; focus your attention       95
as closely as you can on my speech.

Man in his limitation could never
satisfy the terms of redress, for no humbling,
no obedience offered afterward could go

as low as the heights his sin                      100
sought to reach; this is the cause for which
man was unable to satisfy God by himself.

Thus it was up to God in His
own ways to give man his life back,
as I say, with one way or with both.               105

But just as a deed pleases the doer
more, the more it presents the innate
benevolence of the heart, its source,

so the Divine Goodness that imprints
the world, proceeded to move with all              110
His ways to raise you up again.

There has not been nor will be
between the last night and first day, an act
so towering as when He made two ways.

For God revealed greater magnanimity          115
in giving Himself so that man might rise
than if he had simply pronounced pardon.

All other recourse was insufficient
for justice, except for the Son of God
to humble Himself by becoming incarnate.          120

But now, to satisfy all your desires
I go back to revisit one point, so that you
too may appreciate it as plainly as I do.

You say, 'I see that water and fire
and air and earth and all their combinations          125
come to corruption and only briefly endure,

and if these things, also, were created
and if I am to believe what was said before,
why should they be subject to decay?'

Brother, the angels and the true country          130
where you are now—these, we say, were created
just as they are in their whole being,

whereas the elements you spoke of
and all the things that proceed from them are
informed by things that are themselves created.          135

Matter was created, just as within
the stars that fly about us there is a form
that has been fashioned and imparted to them.

The soul of every brute and plant
is pulled forth from a complex potentiality          140
by the motion and sacred light of the stars.

But the Supreme Good inspires
your life immediately to come forth, engendering
such love that the self desires Him always.

And hence you can infer your          145
resurrection, if you think back on how
uniquely human flesh came to be, back

when our first parents appeared."


*Notes*

1–3. "Osanna… malacòth."—a combination of Hebrew and Latin:
"Hosannah, Holy God of armies, lighting from on high these blessed lights,
heaven's souls."
4. as he whirled—i.e., Justinian.

# Canto VIII

[Dante and Beatrice have ascended to the third sphere, that of Venus. Here Dante encounters the souls of the amorous, who came close to losing Heaven by mistaking earthly love for Love. Charles Martel comes forward and explains why God creates morally diverse progeny from the same families.]

To its peril the world once believed
that, wheeling in the third epicycle,
the lovely Cyprian shot wild love rays down

so that ancient nations in ancient error
paid her honor—and not her alone—         5
rendering obeisance in sacrifice and votive cry;

they also honored Dione and Cupid,
one Cyprian's mother, the other her son,
who claimed he had sat on Dido's lap.

And from her with whom I began         10
this canto, they applied her name to the sun-
wooed planet that courts from nape to eyebrow.

I was unaware of my ascent there,
but I reckoned we were inside because
I saw my Lady grow more beautiful.         15

And like a spark made out in a flame,
and as when voice may be discerned inside voice
since one is sostenuto, while the other fluctuates,

so within that light were other lights:
some moving slowly, some more rapidly,         20
but each, I think, according to its inner sense.

Whether visible or not, no cold cloud
ever shot its winds down so rapidly, as not
to seem burdensome and slow

to anyone who saw those divine                         25
lights nearing us, leaving the dance
begun among the high Seraphim;

and from the vanguard there rose
"Hosanna!"—such a sound that I have never
been free of the yearning to hear again.                30

Then one drew close and said,
"We are all here at your pleasure
so that you may derive joy from us."

Ours is one turning and one sphere,
one thirst, as we revolve with the Celestial Princes    35
you once addressed, calling from the world:

'O you, whose intellect turns the third heaven,'
we are so full of love for you that, for your
pleasure, a little pause will be no less pleasing."

I lifted my eyes reverently to meet                     40
those of my Lady, whose own eyes had favored
me with serenity and presence of mind,

and I turned back to the light that
had made such promises to me: "Who are you?"
I said, my voice marked with great affection.           45

And how much greater and brighter
did I behold that spirit grow when, as I
spoke, it took in new joy to add to joy.

Thus changed, it said, "The world
had me a brief time; had it been more,                  50
much future evil would not have been.

My happiness, encompassing me
in its rays, hides me from you: I am enclosed
like an animal swaddled in its own silk.

You loved me greatly once with great                    55
reason, for had I stayed, I would have shown
you more of love than just the leaves.

Washed by waters of the Rhone,
the left bank, when mingled with the Sorgue
awaited me, in due course, to become its lord,        60

as did Ausonia's horn, south of where
the Tronto and Verde disgorge into the sea,
bordered by Catona, Bari, and Gaeta.

Already there flashed on my brow
the crown of the land where the Danube flows          65
once it has abandoned the German borders.

And beautiful Trinacria, whose ashes
along the dark coast between Pachino and Peloro,
ensue from rising sulphur—not Typhoeus,

as stories have it—would nonetheless                   70
have wanted to have its kings descend
through me from Charles and Rudolph,

if despotism, that always dispirits
its subject peoples, had not moved all
Palermo to cry out, 'Death!  Death!'                   75

And if my brother could but foresee
this, he would flee the greedy poverty
of Catalonia, aware it could harry him

for truly, some provision is required
for him or others so that his boat, already           80
burdened, not take on more cargo.

His miserly nature, which descended
from one more generous, made him require
soldiers not be keen on filling their coffers."

"Sire, because I think the lofty delight                           85
your words infuse in me is as clear to you
as to me: there every good begins and ends

and my joy is the greater, and I rejoice
in knowing how you are blessed, since you
perceive it looking into the face of God.                          90

You made me happy; now clear up
a lingering doubt: how it can be that
a sweet seed evolves into a bitter fruit?"

Thus I to him. And he to me:
"If I can make you see just one truth,                              95
then what is behind will appear before you.

The Good that moves and satisfies
all the realm in which you now move renders
providence a power in these great bodies.

For the Mind is not only perfect in itself                         100
but provides for the welfare for every creature
together with its preservation. And thus

whatever arrow flies from this bow
falls to a purposeful end, as surely
as if it were directed to the mark.                                105

If this were not the case, the heaven
through which you fly would provoke chaos,
resulting in ruins, not works of art

and such cannot be, unless the Intellects
that move the stars are flawed and the Original                    110
who made them likewise imperfect.

Would you like me to make the truth
even clearer to you?" And I: "No, I see it is
impossible for nature to refute necessity."

And he once more: "Would it be worse                    115
for earthly man if he were to lose community?"
"Yes," I replied, "I need no further proof."

"And can it be, unless earthly man
lived diversely and followed diverse ends?
Not if the 'no' your master writes is true."                    120

And so, deducing, he came to this
point: "Thus, it behooves the roots of man's
endeavors to have diverse beginnings:

This one is born a Solon; this other,
Xerxes, and this, Melchizedek, and another                    125
who flew through the air and lost the son.

Revolving nature, like a signet ring
to wax, practices her art well, but does not
distinguish one lineage from another.

In the same way, Esau parts with Jacob                    130
in the seed, and Quirinus was born of such a vile
sire that people assumed him a child of Mars.

Generated nature by itself would always
follow the course of the generator, were it not
that Divine Providence intervenes.                    135

What then was behind you is now before:
and because you have so increased my joy
I will bestow one more corollary on you:

should Fortune rise discordantly
with Nature, the result will always be bad,                    140
like any seed, trying to thrive in alien soil.

But if the world below would fix
its resolve on the foundation Nature set out
and begin there, men would be better for it.

But you distort into the priesthood                145
those destined for the sword, and make a king
from one who was meant for sermons: therefore,

your footsteps wander from the road."


*Notes*

3. the lovely Cyprian—Venus.

7. Dione—The mother of Venus.

8–9. the other her son, who claimed he had sat on Dido's lap—In seeming
innocence, Cupid sits on Dido's lap just before she is smitten with Aeneas.

31. Then one drew close—Charles Martel (1271–1295, first son of Charles II of
Anjou.

35. Celestial Princes—Principalities, among the last third of the hierarchy of
angels, including angels and archangels (see XXVIII).

50. a brief time—Charles Martel lived from 1271 to 1295.

55. You loved me greatly—It is assumed that Charles and Dante met and that
Charles promised him patronage.

61. Ausonia's horn—i.e., lower Italy.

67. Trinacria—Sicily ("triangle"), which is volcanic.

69. Typhoeus—In Greek myth, a deadly giant, the offspring of Gaia and Tartarus.

75. moved all Palermo to cry out—i.e., The Sicilian Vespers, the uprising against
the rule of the Frenchman Charles I, so named because it began on the evening
vigil of Easter Monday, 1282.

76. And if my brother—Robert, Charles' brother, who succeeded their father in
1309. Catalonian officials were reputed to be miserly.

123–124. Solon; this other, Xerxes, and this, Melchizedek—i.e., the type,
respectively, of a lawgiver, a military leader, and a high priest.

130. Quirinus—i.e., Romulus.

# Canto IX

[Dante meets Cunizza, who prophecies dark things for her native Venice for pursuing self-interest. She is succeeded by Folquet, another of the amorous, who averted his own carnal desires to discover the True Love and gives Dante a disquisition on the nature of the third sphere. Finally, Rahab inveighs against the sins of Boniface VIII, Dante's Papal foe.]

Once your Charles had pronounced,
Fair Clemence, his enlightening words, he then
foretold future conspiracies against my seed.

He said, "Say nothing, let the years
turn." I can only say that those who harm          5
you will smart from justice and pay in tears.

Now the life of that sacred light
turned toward the sun that fills it, just
as to the good that satisfies all things.

Ah, hoodwinked souls, faithless beings,          10
who avert your hearts from such good
and bend your brows toward emptiness!

And then another of those splendid lights
moved in my direction, and by turning up
its brightness showed its will to please me.          15

The eyes of Beatrice that fastened
on me, as before, gave me full assurance
that my desire met her approval.

"O blessed spirit," I said, "requite
my wish and show me proof that you          20
can be the mirror of what I think."

At this, the light of one still unrecognized,
singing from out from the depths, answered
like one whose joy was joyfulness itself.

"In that corrupt part of Italy                          25
that lies between the Rialto and the springs
from which the Brenta and Piava rivers flow

rises an unexceptional hill from which
some time ago a warrior descended
and put the countryside to the torch.                   30

Both he and I share the same root.
I was called Cunizza, and I shine here
because this star's light overcame me.

But I gladly forgive myself the thing
that caused my fate: it doesn't discourage me,          35
which might seem strange to ordinary minds.

Of the spectacular jewel that dazzles
here, nearest me, so great fame remains
that before it dies, the centennial year

will have been quintupled. Now see                      40
if you oughtn't make man an excellent thing
so that a second life surpass the first.

This will signify nothing to the masses
who teem between Tagliamento and Adige,
nor does the whip render them repentant.                45

But soon will it be that marshy Padua
will turn the water bloody that flows to Vicenza
where the people, who shunned their duty, bathe.

And where the Sile and Cagnan meet
there rules one who carries his head high               50
for whom a spider web is being prepared.

Feltro shall yet wail for the treachery
of her unholy crime, for none was ever yet
sentenced to Malta for such an offense.

Indeed, a tank large enough to hold          55
Ferrara's blood would be colossal, and the man
wasted who would weigh it by the ounce.

All this the courteous priest
would sacrifice to show his partisan colors,
but such gifts reflect that country's customs.          60

Above are mirrors, what you call Thrones,
from which God's judgments shine down on us,
giving grounds for us to speak this way.

She fell silent then and seemed
to turn away to other things, resuming her place          65
in the turning dance where she had been before.

That other joy, already known
to me as precious to her, then came
into my sight like a fine, sun-struck ruby.

On high, joy is brightness, just as          70
here, on earth, we smile; but lower down
the darkening shades register desolation.

"God sees everything, O Blessed Spirit,"
I said, "and your sight works through Him,
so that no desire can ever hide itself.          75

So your voice, which has always
made Heaven glad with singing, as those
Holy Flames make a cowl of their six wings,

why does it not sate my longings?
If I had the power to know your wishes as you          80
have mine, I would not hesitate so."

And with these words he began,
"The widest basin into which water spills
from sea-girdled earth extends so far

between opposed strands, and against        85
the eastern sun, that when it reaches
the meridian that place is also its horizon.

I lived along the shore of that valley
between Ebro and Magra, whose abbreviated
course divides Tuscans and Genoese.        90

Bougie and my city share virtually
the same sunset and dawn; its harbor
once was heated by its people's blood.

To those who knew me, my name
was Folquet, this sphere now imprints itself      95
with me, as I once felt its imprint at my birth

for even Dido, daughter of Belus,
who wronged both Sichaeus and Creusa,
never burned as I, till my hair turned sere,

nor did the Rhodopean woman        100
whom Demophoön deceived, nor Hercules
when he locked Iole within his heart.

But here none repents; instead we smile,
not at the fault, where the mind no longer goes,
but at the ordering and visionary Power.      105

It's here we behold that art graced
with such love that we can discern the Good
through which the upper world turns the lower.

But so that all of your cravings
born of this sphere are fully satisfied,      110
let me proceed. You want to know

who is in this light that shines
so brilliantly here beside me, as
a sunbeam suspended in pellucid water.

Then know that inside there Rahab                    115
is at peace, and since joined with our order,
she seals it in the highest degree.

To this sphere, where the shadow
of earth has its end, Rahab came as the first
of the souls led upward in Christ's triumph.         120

It was fitting that she be admitted
to this heaven, trophy of the high victory
won for us by those two palms,

for it was she who made Joshua's
first victory in the Holy Land possible,             125
a fact absent from the Pope's memory.

Your city, planted by him who
first turned his back on his Maker,
and whose envy cost us untold mourning,

brings forth and strews an evil flower,              130
transforms shepherds into starved wolves,
driving lambs and sheep from the fold.

And so the Gospel and the Church
Doctors are derelict, and only Canon Law
is studied, as the margins attest.                   135

On this the Pope and Cardinals focus;
their thoughts do not extend to Nazareth,
where Gabriel opened his wings.

But the Vatican and other chosen
places of Rome, which have been burial grounds       140
for soldiers who followed Peter,

will soon be rid of this adultery.

## Notes

1. Fair Clemence—It is unclear which Clemence the poet is addressing. One candidate is the wife of Charles Martel, who died in 1295, just as her husband did. The other candidate is the daughter of Charles Martel, Clemence of Anjou, who was alive at the time of this address.

13. another of those splendid lights—Cunizza (see below).

24. that corrupt part of Italy—Venezia.

28. a warrior—Enzolino, Cunizza's brother.

31. Cunizza—Cunizza de Romano (1198–1279), daughter of Ezzolino II, Count of Onora, who appears in Hell (*Inferno* XII). She was known for her carnal disposition, including a liaison with the Troubadour Sordello. Although she set free slaves who had been in bondage to her father, it is not altogether clear why she is in heaven or why she delivers a prophecy.

36. the spectacular jewel—Folquet de Marselha (1150–1231), troubadour poet, crusader against the Albigensians, and Cistercian monk. He initiated what became the Dominican Order.

47. the people, who shunned their duty—They (Paduans) presumably shunned the duty they owed to Dante's patron, Can Grande, the Ghibelline leader.

49. there rules one—Rizzardo da Cammino, Lord of Treviso (1274–1312. He was murdered while playing chess with Alteniero degli Azzoni, whose wife Rizzardo had seduced.

51. Feltro—Allesandro Novella, Bishop of Feltro (1250–1320). Accepting a group of Ghibelline refugees, he turned them over to an agent of Robert of Naples, who had them beheaded in public. Dishonored, Feltro retreated to a monastery, where he died in 1320.

53. for none was ever yet sentenced to Malta—a prison on an island in Lake Bolsena.

55. Ferrara's blood—Feltro's victims, Ghibellines, were largely from Ferrara.

66. That other joy—i.e., Folquet.

90. Bougie—(now Béjaïa) in Algeria. Bougie has a similar longitude to Marseilles.

96. Dido—In the Aeneid, Dido, Queen of Carthage, falls madly in love with Aeneas. After her suicide, she reunites with her former husband Sychaeus in Hades, where Aeneas encounters them. Creusa was Aeneas' wife, who died as Aeneas left Troy. He encounters her ghost as he is leaving.

99. The Rhodopean woman whom Demophoön, son of Theseus, deceived— Phyllis, daughter of King Sithon of Thrace was abandoned by her groom on her wedding day, whereupon she hanged herself. (Ovid, *Heroides II* 147–48)

118. Rahab—A prostitute who helped Joshua's spies to escape the king (Joshua II). In doing so, she helped the Israelites to achieve the promised land, and her soul ascended to heaven after the crucifixion.

125. the Pope's memory—that of Boniface VIII.

126. him—Satan.

136–137. Nazareth, where Gabriel opened his wings—i.e., at the Annunciation.

# Canto X

[Dante and Beatrice rise to the sphere of the Sun (the fourth sphere), where he meets the Doctors of the Church, who are introduced by Saint Thomas Aquinas.]

Contemplating His Son with the love
that each of them breathes always,
the great and ineffable Original has created

everything in mind and space
with such order that whoever encounters                    5
that harmony can't fail to behold His presence.

So raise your vision, reader, to the great
wheels and look straight toward the part
where the one motion strikes the other.

And there begin to contemplate                             10
the Master who so loves his work
that his eye is forever fixed there.

Behold next how the oblique circle
branching from that point carries the planets
to satisfy the earth that calls to them.                   15

If that star road were not slanted
the heavenly virtues would be in vain
and nearly all power here below—dead,

and if that track departed a little
more or a little less from its course,                     20
both hemispheres would suffer disorder.

Now, reader, don't leave the table,
think of your delight in the foretaste,
consider how you hope to dine before retiring.

I have prepared your fare, now eat                            25
because the matter of which I am the scribe
calls now for my complete attention.

The greatest Minister of nature,
who imprints earth with heaven's hallmark
and measures time with light, now                             30

in conjunction with that part I
showed you, was riding those spirals
that make him appear earlier each day.

And I was with him, the sun,
but no more conscious of soaring upward                       35
than one is of an abrupt thought's arrival.

It is Beatrice who guides our flight
going from good to better so suddenly
that time has no way of measuring it.

How brilliant were the lights                                 40
I saw on entering the sun; I knew them
not by color, but by their manifest glory.

Even if I called upon genius, art,
and custom, I could not get you to imagine;
you must believe and long to see.                             45

If our fantasies are too base
to attain such a height, no wonder: the eye
has never met a brightness beyond sunlight.

Such was the fourth sphere
where the High Father, always fulfilling,                     50
shows how He breathes and engenders.

And Beatrice: "Give thanks
to the Sun of the Angels, by whose grace
you have been raised to this physical one."

Never was a mortal heart                                55
so disposed to Godly devotion, to yield
so wholly to Love in willing gratitude

as mine was at those words
and so committed to the giving of that love
that Beatrice was eclipsed and put from mind.           60

Nor was she displeased but smiled
and her eyes laughed at the splendor,
returning my mind to its divided view.

I saw living flashes in which we
formed a center, and they a crown, with voices          65
sweeter in sound than light in brilliance.

It's just as with Latona's daughter
who, when the air is full and holds the thread,
makes about her a halo of woven air.

In Heaven's court, from which I                          70
have returned, such precious gems exist
that they cannot be taken from that realm,

and those singing lights were one.
Whoever does not take wing to reach that kingdom
must await tidings from the mute here below.            75

After those ardent suns, while still singing,
had circled us three times, even as those
wheeling stars close to the fixed poles,

they seemed to me like ladies
who had just paused in dancing, listening               80
for the next notes to begin their steps again

and from within one light I heard a voice:
"Since grace is the kindling of true love, love
itself grows accordingly the more it loves,

grows, shines in splendor                                                      85
and increases, leading you up a ladder where
none goes down who does not ascend again.

Whoever should withhold his wine
from your thirst would be no more free
than clogged water bound for the sea.                                          90

You would like to know what plants
knit the garland that circles that beautiful lady
who gives you strength for Heaven.

I was a lamb of the holy flock
that Dominic leads down his path, where                                        95
one, if he did not stray, would fatten.

This one nearest to my right
was both brother and my master: Albert
of Cologne, and I am Thomas of Aquino.

If you would like to know all                                                  100
the others, then follow my speech as it comes
to each face turning on this blessed wreath.

The next flame is that of the smile
of Gratian, who served two courts of law so well
that it pleases Paradise to welcome him.                                       105

The other, who adorns our choir
was that Peter, who, like the poor widow,
offered his treasure to the Holy Church.

The fifth and most beautiful light
among us inspires such love that the world                                     110
down below yearns for tidings of it.

His flame enfolds a mind so deep
in its wisdom that if truth is true, never
could a second have arisen. Next you see

the flame of that candle, who,                           115
when it inhabited flesh below, peered most
within the nature of angels and their ministry.

Out of that small candle comes
the smile of an advocate from Christian times
who, out of his Latin, furnished Augustine.             120

Now if your mind has followed
my praise from light to light you will be keen
to know who shines in the eighth flame.

The holy soul rejoices to know
the good that lives within and reveals                   125
the world's deception to any who would hear.

The body from which it was evicted
lies down in Cieldauro, and it was from
martyrdom and exile that he came to this place.

Farther on you see flame that is                         130
the urgent breath of Isadore, of Bede, and Richard
who in contemplation was more than man.

The light from which you return
your attention is the light of that one grave
spirit who deemed that death came too slowly.           135

It is the eternal light of Sigir, who lectured
on the Street of Straw, revealing in syllogisms
awkward truths that earned him resentment."

Then like the clock intoning the hour
when the Bride of God is roused to sing                  140
matins to the Bridegroom to further his love

each part to the other pulls and thrusts
in tintinnabulations so sweet that the willing
soul feels the spirit of love surging.

So I witnessed the rotation of that glorious          145
wheel that moved and sang voice to voice
with such sweetness and harmony as to be

unknowable, except where joy meets the eternal.


*Notes*

28. The greatest Minister of nature—i.e., the sun.

67. Latona's daughter—i.e., the moon.

82. I heard a voice—The speaker is St. Thomas Aquinas (1227–1274), author of *Summa Theologica*, preeminent philosopher of the Middle Ages and main source of Dante's theology.

97. This one—Aquinas begins introducing Doctors of the Church, a Catholic designation of persons of exceptional talent in theology.

98–99. Albert of Cologne—Albertus Magnus (1200–1280), bishop and philosopher.

104. Gratian—twelfth century scholar, author of *Concordia discordantium canonum*, a work of canonical law, synthesizing ecclesiastical and civil law.

107. Peter—Petrus Lombardus, Bishop of Paris (d. 1160). His work, *Sententiarum Libri IV*, a collection of texts of the Church Fathers. His work Dante compares as parallel to that of Gratian.

109. the fifth and most beautiful light—Solomon, whose Song of Songs was considered a wedding hymn of the Church and God.

115. the flame of that candle—Dionysus the Areopagite, a judge who, in Acts (12:34), was converted to Christianity by the Apostle Paul.

120. Augustine—St. Augustine (354–430), author of *Civitatis Dei* (*The City of God*), *Confessions*, and other works of enduring influence.

123. the eighth flame—Boethius (ca. 470–524). His *Consolation of Philosophy*, was written as he was awaiting execution.

128. Cieldauro—Church of St. Peter in Pavia, where Boethius' remains were interred.

130. Isadore—Isadore of Seville (ca. 560–636), Archbishop of Seville and Doctor of the Church. Author of *Etymologie*, an encyclopedia of classical learning.

130. Bede—The Venerable Bede (ca. 672–735), historian. Declared a Doctor of the Church by Pope Leo XIII.

130. Richard—Richard of St. Victor (d. circa 1173), Scottish philosopher. Called The Great Contemplator.

136. Siger—Siger of Brabant (ca. 1240–ca. 1284), philosopher, University of Paris. He was cited for heresy by the Grand Inquisitor of France for his teachings and fled to Orvieto, where he was stabbed to death by his secretary.

137. Street of Straw—at the University of Paris (rue du Fouarre), the site of open-air classes.

# Canto XI

[Aquinas continues by describing the life and holiness of St. Francis, then explains the relationship between the Franciscans and the Dominicans and ends by denouncing of the degradation of the Dominicans.]

O senseless struggles of mortality;
how shoddy your syllogisms are that make
you flap your wings to soar downward!

One studied law and one the Aphorisms;
one followed the priesthood, and one           5
how to rule by either force or fraud;

some stole; others conducted state affairs;
some chased after amusements of the flesh;
still others succumbed to indolence;

and I, released from such things,           10
was with Beatrice there high in Heaven
where I was approved and welcomed.

When each light came round again
returning to where it had been before, it
stopped as still as a candle in a chandelier.      15

And inside the splendor that had spoken
before I heard words commence again,
and as it smiled, its brightness surged.

"Just as my light is kindled in His,
so, as I gaze into that Eternal light, I can      20
understand the measure of your thoughts.

You are in doubt, and you want me
to explain to you in clear, simple language
that satisfies your grasp of two points,

where I earlier said, 'where one          25
fattens well' and 'a second never arose':
I must make a crucial distinction.

The world-governing Providence
whose wisdom is so profound that Its
creatures can never plumb its depths,          30

so that the Groom, crying aloud,
and taking her in marriage with His consecrated
blood, might better answer the Beloved

self-confident and faithful,
ordained two princes to attend her          35
on either side and to guide her.

One was seraphic in his ardor,
the other by virtue of his wisdom was
a splendor of cherubic brilliance on earth.

I will devote my narrative to one          40
prince, for in praising either, I praise
both, as they work toward the same end.

Between Tupino and the water
that descends the hill blessed Ubaldo chose,
a fertile slope hangs from a high mountain.          45

Perugia feels the heat and cold
that blows through Porta Sole, and behind it
Gualdo and Nocera grieve for their heavy yoke.

On that slope, there where
the steepness breaks, rose a sun, just as          50
this one rises sometimes from the Ganges.

Therefore, of the ways to call this place,
let no one say 'Ascesi,' as being too limited,
but Orient, if he would speak properly.

It wasn't far from his rising 55
when the sun began to make the earth
take some comfort from his strength.

Even as a youth he went against
his father on behalf of a lady, to whom
all would bar the door, as if to death itself. 60

And before the spiritual court
and his father he wed Lady Poverty
and loved her more and more each day.

Deprived of her first husband,
she had no suitor for eleven centuries 65
and lived in that way until he came.

Not even when forceful men
found her fearless and calm, like Amyclas,
secure against the voice of power.

And not even when, loyal 70
and unafraid, with Mary remaining below,
she climbed upon the cross to be with Christ.

I do not wish to speak so darkly.
You understand I mean Francis and Poverty
who are meant to be lovers in this tale. 75

Their concord and radiant looks,
their love, wonder and tender mutual care
gave birth to thoughts of pure devotion.

So much so that the venerable one
immediately bared his feet, and though racing 80
for peace, judged his gait too plodding.

O unknown wealth! O fruitful Good!
Giles goes unshodden; likewise Sylvester,
so loving the bride they seek the bridegroom.

Then that father, that master, set                    85
forth with his wife and that family, which was
now wearing the humble cord for belt.

No shame weighed on his heart
at being born the son of Pietro Bernadone,
not for the scorn and wonder occasioned.              90

But like a king he disclosed
his rigid determination to Innocent
who presented the seal to his Order.

After the mendicants swelled
behind this man, whose exemplary life                 95
were better sung in the glory of Heaven,

a second crown was bestowed
by the Eternal Spirit through Honorius
the divine purpose of this Archimandrite,

and then, in his thirst for martyrdom,                100
in the presence of the pompous sultan
he preached Christ and His followers.

But finding the people unripe
for conversion, and not wishing to preach
in vain, he returned to harvest Italian fields.       105

On a rugged rock between Tiber
and Arno he received the final imprimatur,
Christ's wounds that showed for two years.

When He who ordained him
to such goodness wished to draw him up                110
to the reward his humility earned him,

and then to his brothers, as to
his rightful heirs, he commended his lady
and instructed them to love her faithfully;

and in returning to his kingdom,                        115
he wished his celebrated soul parted from
her bosom, and for his body no further bier.

    Now think about the kind of man
was worthy to be a colleague who could
keep Peter's boat steady on the sea.                    120

    Such a man was our Patriarch,
and so you see with what good cargo he
is freighted, who follows his commands.

    But now his flock grows so greedy
that it wanders off into strange, remote               125
pastures in search of novel food

    and as his sheep, distant vagabonds,
stray even farther, the less milk they bring
back to the fold when they return.

    There are some afraid enough                       130
to stay near the shepherd, but so few that
to make their cowls would take little cloth.

    Now if my words have not been
garbled, and if you have listened attentively,
and if you remember my former words,                   135

    in part your wishes will have been
satisfied and you will see how the tree
is chipped and why I argued that if

    they do not stray, 'all may fatten.'"

## Notes

4. Aphorisms—of Hippocrates (460–370 B.C.), a study of medicine.

36. two princes—St. Dominic and St. Francis.

45. blessed Ubaldo—St. Ubaldo (1084–1160), Bishop of Gubbio, who intended a hermitage near Gubbio.

54. let no one say 'Ascesi'—i.e, "I have risen." Also Assisi.

60. a lady—Lady Poverty.

69. Amyclas—a fisherman (Convivio IV, 13) who, in his poverty, lay fearlessly on a bed of seaweed before Caesar.

84. Giles—Blessed Giles of Assisi (1190–1262), an early follower of St. Francis.

84. Sylvester—Sylvester of Assisi (c. 1175–1240), another early disciple of St. Francis.

86-87. Then that father, that master, set forth with his wife and that family— i.e., Francis, Lady Poverty and disciples.

90. Pietro Bernadone—St. Francis' father was a wealthy silk merchant.

104. Honorius—Pope Honorius III (1150–1227) approved the Franciscan Order in 1223.

105. Archimandrite—i.e., a priest one rank lower than Bishop.

114. Christ's wounds—Tradition holds that Francis bore the stigmata.

# Canto XII

[Dante meets the soul of St. Bonaventure, who praises the Franciscan Order, but like Aquinas in the previous canto, also notes the slippage of the order.]

No sooner had that blessed flame
uttered his last word than the holy
millstone resumed its rotation.

But it had not completed a single
turn before it was joined by another wheel          5
matching it motion for motion, song for song,

singing that transcended the strains
of either the Sirens or the Muses, as original
splendor outshines any reflection.

Just like two rainbows arcing down          10
from a cloud, alike in color and parallel,
Juno giving commands to her handmaid

the outer born of the inner,
like the voice of that one whom love
had separated, like dew from the sun,          15

they let the people here know
of the covenant God made with Noah,
that the world need not fear another flood.

Thus it was those everlasting roses
wove two garlands about us and the outer          20
one answered to the inner one's call.

Then the dancing, and that grand
festa, both with singing and radiance
upon gleaming radiance, joyous and gentle

and then as if in agreement, they                25
fell instantly still (just as our eyes do,
opening and closing with a single will).

From the heart of one
of the new lights came a voice and I
turned like a needle to a star.                  30

And he said, "The love that beautifies
moves me to speak of that other leader,
who is the reason I am well spoken of here.

It is proper to name one with
the other, for they fought side by side          35
and so may share that bright glory.

The Christian soldiers, so costly
to rearm, slogged behind their standard
and marched slowly, irresolute, and few

when the Emperor, who reigns                      40
eternally, supplied his imperiled troops
by grace alone, not by merit. And then,

as was said, He sent His Bride
two champions who rescued the straggling
company and, by example, revived them.           45

In that part where sweet Zephyr
swells to open the new leaves of which
Europe is seen to clothe itself,

not very far from the waves
behind which the sun, in its long course,        50
hides itself at times from every man,

lies fortunate Calahorra under
the aegis of a mighty shield that displays
two lions: one subject, one sovereign.

There was born an fervent                               55
lover of the Christian faith, a holy athlete ,
benign to his own, severe to enemies.

As soon as he was conceived
his mind swelled with such overflowing
power in her womb she could prophesy.                   60

As soon as the ritual of marriage
was completed at the holy font, he and his Faith
pledged each other eternal salvation.

The lady who had given assent
for him saw in a dream the miraculous fruit             65
that would issue from his lineage.

And so that his name might signify
what he was, a Heavenly spirit was moved
to name him in His possessive, as he was

so entrusted. He was called Dominic;                    70
I refer to that husbandman whom Christ
elected to help Him work His garden.

A fitting envoy and servant of Christ,
he made it evident that his first love was love
for the first directive that Christ gave.               75

Often he was found by his nurse
lying awake and meditative on the ground
as if to say, "this is what I have come for."

O you, father Felix, well named!
O you, his mother, Joanna, equally graced,              80
if these names mean what they suggest!

Not for the world nor its profit
in studying the Ostian or Thaddeus,
but for love of the true manna,

he soon became a great Doctor,                           85
making his rounds in that vineyard that soon
withers, if the vintner neglects his task.

And from the seat, once favorable
to the worthy poor (not through itself, thanks
to its occupant, who sits there debased)                  90

he did not give out two or three
for six, nor ask for some prime vacancy
nor *decimas, quae sunt pauperum Dei*,

but lobbied for the mission to battle
an errant world for the seed from which grew              95
the two dozen plants surrounding you.

Then armed with doctrine and will,
and with apostolic warrant, he moved
like a mountain flood crashing down

until with greatest impact he struck                     100
where the shoots of heresy were thickest
and most resistant. And from him

there sprang a delta of steams
by which the catholic fields are fed to make
sure its saplings have a verdant life.                   105

If he was one wheel of the chariot
the Holy Church used to defend itself
and win on the field of civil conflict;

well may you understand then
the excellence of the other, to whom Thomas              110
was so courteous before my coming.

But now the outer rim of that cask's
circumference has been neglected so there
is mold now where once there was crust.

His family, who once traced                            115
his steps, have now become so reversed
that the front foot now follows the back.

And soon you will see the resulting
harvest of this inept husbandry, when tares
will bemoan right of access to the granary.            120

And yet I must admit that if one
were to search leaf by leaf through our book
he would still find 'I am what I always was.'

The same cannot be said of those
who come from Casal or Aquiparta, who read            125
the word either too narrowly, or too freely.

I am the soul of Bonaventure
of Bagnoregio, who in my offices
always put by cares of lesser worth.

Illuminato and Augustine are here                      130
who were the first barefooted brethren
who became friends of God and wore the cord.

Hugh of Saint Victor is among them,
with Peter Mangiadore and Peter of Spain
whose twelve books shine below,                        135

Nathan the Prophet, the Metropolitan
Chrysostom, Anselm, and that Donatus
who turned a worthy hand to the first art.

Rabanus is here, and at my side
shines the Calabrian abbot Joachim, who                140
was endowed with the spirit of prophecy.

To celebrate so great a paladin
I am led by the bright courtesy of Thomas
whose discerning Latin stirred me

and those who have joined this company."               145

## Notes

1. that blessed flame—i.e., St. Thomas Aquinas.

129. one of the new lights—St. Bonaventure (1221–1274), theologian, and General of the Franciscan Order (1257). He was made Cardinal in 1273. He was named by Pope Sixtus IV (1414–1484) as among the Doctors of the Church.

32. that other leader—St. Dominic (1170–1221), founder of the Dominican Order. Dominic founded the order in part to divert the Albigensian sect from their heresy.

35. they fought side by side—i.e., Francis and Dominic.

52. Calahorra—birthplace in Spain of St. Dominic.

53. aegis of a mighty shield—the House of Castille.

79. Felix, well named—i.e., "happy."

80. Joanna— i.e., "gracious."

83. Ostian—Enrico di Susa became Bishop of Ostia (1271) and scholar of canon law.

83. Thaddeus—Taddeo d'Alderotto, (born 1125), a celebrated Florentine physician who founded the college of medicine at the University of Bologna.

93. *non decimas, quae sunt pauperum Dei* —"not the tithes, which belong to the poor of God."

110. Thomas—i.e., Thomas Aquinas.

130. Casal or Aquiparta—The first a Franciscan monastery in Casale in Monferato. Its general, Ubertino di Casale (1259–1338, tightened the rule; the second, Matteo d' Aquasparta (1240–1302), general of the monastery in Todi, relaxed the Franciscan rule.

132–133. Bonaventure—Bonaventure of Bagnoregio, theologian. Canonized and made a Doctor of the Church by Sixtus in 1558, Bonaventure studied at the University of Paris and graduated with Thomas Aquinas. A Franciscan, he was Minister General of the Order of Friars Minor.

135. Illuminato and Augustine—two early Franciscans.

138. Hugh of Saint Victor—(ca. 1196–1141) taught philosophy at the monastery of St. Victor in Paris.

139. Peter Mangiadore—(1110–1179) Dean of the Cathedral of Troyes. Peter wrote *Historia Scholastica*, long an authoritative text on Biblical history.

139. Peter of Spain—(1215–1277), a physician, author of *Summulae Logicales*. He became Pope John XXI in 1276.

140. Nathan the Prophet—See II Samuel, xii. Nathan railed against the sins of King David.

141. Metropolitan Chrysostom—John of Antioch (ca. 344–407), Metropolitan of Constantinople. Like Nathan, he denounced the ruler (Empress Eudoxia).

142. Anselm—Anselm of Canterbury, Archbishop (ca. 1033–1109). He fought with both King William II and Henry I over Church authority, for which he was twice exiled.

142. Donatus—Fourth century grammarian, whose book on grammar was widely used in Dante's time. He also wrote commentaries on Terence and Virgil.

144. Rabanus—Rabanus Maurus Magnentius (ca. 780-856), Archbishop of Mainz, wide-ranging Biblical scholar and grammarian, he was called the "teacher of Germany."

145. the Calabrian abbot Joachim—Of Fiore (ca. 1132–1202), theologian and mystic. A Cistercian, his interpretive and prophetic works were well known during Dante's time.

147. paladin—The "paladins" were originally twelve champions who surrounded Charlemagne.

148. Thomas—i.e., Thomas Aquinas.

# Canto XIII

[Dante rhapsodizes about the two heavenly circles of souls that make up a double garland of dancers and compares them to constellations. Aquinas, reading Dante's mind, explains the wisdom of Solomon.]


Imagine, if you would understand
the thing I saw (and hold the image
rock-steady in your mind while I speak it):

the fifteen brightest stars in heaven
that quicken the firmament with such a glow          5
it can pierce the thickest fog;

imagine then the Wain that lies
day and night on heaven's breast so that
when the pole turns, it never sinks;

imagine further the mouth of the horn          10
that begins at the tip of that axis
in which the Primum Mobile turns

forming two constellations,
like that Minos' daughter made in the sky
when she first felt the chill of death;          15

one's rays within the other
shining in coordinated orbit, one
going forward, the other in reverse,

and you will have some idea
of the truth of that constellation and the double          20
dance that circled the point where I was,

because it surpasses sense
as much as the motion of the fastest
sphere outruns the current of Chiana.

They sang no Bacchic or Paean there                25
but of the three Persons in divine nature,
and in one Person divine and human.

The circling and singing reached
their measure, and those holy lights turned
happily to us, as they ranged care to care.        30

The silence of the concord was
broken by the same light which had told
the admirable story of God's pauper

and said, "Since one sheaf
is threshed and its grain in the granary,           35
sweet love leads me to thresh the other one.

You think that into that breast
where a rib was drawn that formed the face
whose taste was to cost mankind so dearly,

and into the One who by the lance                   40
gave past and future such satisfaction
that it outweighed every fault,

whatever of light has been permitted
human nature to have was infused by
the same power that created them both;              45

and so you were surprised at
what I said earlier that no other possessed
the good surrounding our fifth light.

Now open your eyes at my answer,
believe, and you will see your belief               50
and my words fit like the center of a circle.

Both that which dies and that which
does not die are just the splendor of the Idea
which our Lord creates by His love

that living light that pours from                              55
its shining spring yet never leaves it,
nor from the thrice-united Love,

for His goodness gathers its rays
as in a mirror, through nine subsistent
orders, though remaining eternally One.                         60

Then it descends to the last power
from act to act, dwindling to the point
where it can only bring forth brief events;

I count these contingencies
to be generated things, things produced                         65
by heavenly motion from seed or not.

The wax and what shapes the wax
are changeable, and so the Idea's seal radiates
through sometimes more, sometimes less.

Thus within the same species                                    70
some trees bear better fruit, some worse,
and men are born with different characters.

If the wax were perfectly rendered
and the heavens at the utmost of their virtú
the seal's radiance would beam forth                            75

but nature is deficient
like an artist skilled at what he does
but whose hand shakes. And yet,

if the intense Love moves
the Primal Power to supreme clarity,                            80
then its seal is absolutely perfect.

It was in this way that earth
was created worthy of animal perfection;
thus was the Virgin made pregnant.

So I do commend your opinion                    85
that human nature has never been, nor
ever will be, what it was in those two.

Now if I were to stop there
you would immediately ask, "How can
you say the other has no match?"                90

But to clarify what seems still
unclear, think who he was and what
the occasion when he was told, "Ask."

I have spoken so that you
can see clearly he was a king who asked          95
for sufficient wisdom to rule worthily,

not in order to enumerate
and group the angels or know whether
you can get a "must" from a "may" in logic,

nor *si est dare primum motum esse*,             100
nor if you can draw a triangle without
a right angle within a semicircle.

So when I talked of wisdom
it was royal prudence at which
the arrow of my intention was drawn.             105

And if you look at the word
"arose," you will see I meant only kings,
who are many, though good ones rare.

If you take properly what I say,
you will find it consistent with your belief     110
in our first father and our delight.

This will be lead to your steps
to make you move slowly, like a man
weary of the unseen yes and no,

for whoever decides without                                    115
distinguishing, whether affirming or denying
is among the most abysmal of fools.

   Hasty opinions can often lead
one the wrong way, and then affection
for one's own viewpoint ties up the intellect.               120

   He is worse than useless who leaves
shore to fish for truth but lacks skill;
he returns worse off than when he left.

   Parmenides, Melissus, and Bryson
are clear proofs of this, and others,                          125
who went about without knowing where.

   And so did Sabellus and Arius
whose concave sword blades distorted
the straight face of the Scriptures.

   Men should not be too confident                 130
in their judgments; they are like those
who prize a field of corn before it is ripe.

   For I have seen the stiff and piercing
briar stem all winter long show its thorn, when
it would later hold up, on its top, a rose,                    135

   and I once saw a ship sail straight
and fast on its journey across the sea
only to perish at the mouth of the harbor.

   Let not Mr. He and Miss She think
when they see one thieving, another giving alms               140
they are looking through Divine eyes,

   for one may rise, the other fall."

## Notes

7. Wain—i.e., the Big Dipper.

10. the horn—the Little Dipper.

12. Primum Mobile—the Primum Mobile ("prime mover")—the outermost sphere whose turning moves the other spheres.

14. Minos' daughter—Ariadne. Abandoned by Theseus, she was taken to heaven by Dionysus, who gave her the constellation Corona Borealis as her wreath.

24. Chiana—a sluggish river in Tuscany and Umbria.

25. no Bacchic or Paean—i.e., no song such as the pagans sang of Dionysus (Bacchic) or Apollo (Paean).

32. the same light—i.e., Aquinas.

33. God's pauper— i.e., St. Francis.

36. to thresh the other one—In the metaphor of threshing, Dante's "straw" is (again) separated from the grain (the truth), first about the truth of the Franciscans and Dominicans and here as it pertains to the wisdom of Solomon.

53. the splendor of the Idea—i.e., the image of the idea.

105. nor *si est dare primum motum esse*—"Nor, whether a prime motion is to be admitted" (i.e., without cause).

116. our first father and our delight—i.e., Adam and Christ.

129. Parmenides—early Greek philosopher, proponent of the view that all reality was One.

129. Melissus—Greek philosopher, follower of Parmenides.

129. Bryson—an early Greek philosopher who appears in Aristotle as having tried fraudulently to square the circle.

132. Sabellus—North African (d. ca. 265) heresiarch who refused to accept the Trinity.

132. Arius—(d. 336), founder of the Arian heresy (that Father and Son are not of one substance).

# Canto XIV

[In the presence of the double garland of souls, Dante asks for an explanation of the resurrection of the flesh. Solomon answers. Now aware of a third ring of lights, Dante and Beatrice ascend to the fifth sphere, that of Mars, where he witnesses the Cross as a series of moving lights and from which emanates a sublime hymn.]

Water in a round container will move
from center to rim when struck within
and from rim to center when struck without.

This image suddenly dropped into my mind
as soon as the glorious, living light of Thomas          5
had finished enlightening with his word,

because a similarity appeared between
his discourse and the words of Beatrice,
and she began to speak when he stopped:

"This man, though he does not tell          10
you of it, nor does he think it yet, must
locate the root of still another truth.

Tell him if the light by which
your substance flourishes will shine
from you eternally, just as it does now.          15

And if it so, then explain how,
once your eyes have been restored, you
can bear such intensity and not be harmed.

Just as dancers in a ring pick up
the beat when greater joy overtakes them          20
step more lively and raise their voices,

So at her prompt and devout entreaty,
the holy circles displayed new joy
in turning dance and miraculous song.

     Whoever would complain because          25
we die down there to live up here has never
felt the freshening of God's eternal rain.

     That One, Two and Three who lives
and reigns always and Three, Two and One,
non-circumscribed yet all-circumscribing          30

     was sung three times by all
the spirits with a such melody that it
would be for every merit a fitting reward.

     And I heard in the smaller circle
of that divine light a modest voice          35
perhaps like that of the angel to Mary,

     reply, "As long as the feast
of Paradise will be, so will our love
be clothed in such a radiance.

     Our brilliance arises in proportion          40
to our love, our love to our vision, and that
to the portion of grace that succeeds it.

     When glorified and sanctified,
and our flesh once again clothed in spirit
it will be the more pleasing, being complete          45

     and therefore the light given
us already by the Highest Good is augmented
by the light that allows us to see Him.

     Thus, vision must increase
along with the ardor that the vision kindles          50
and the brilliance the ardor rouses.

     But just as coal burns white,
its inner glow exceeding its outer flame
so that it maintains its appearance,

so will the radiance that encloses　　　　　55
us be surpassed by renewed flesh
that the diurnal earth now covers.

Nor will such bright light be
hard to bear, for our organs will have
strengthened to undertake all our joys.　　60

So quick and zealous were
both choirs to say, "Amen!" that they showed
how they longed to have bodies back,

perhaps not even for themselves,
but for their mothers, fathers, and all their　　65
dear ones before they became eternal flames.

And behold, all around
with equal brightness there arose a light
the way the horizon comes on at dawn.

And even as at dusk new lights　　　　　70
begin to appear in the sky, so that the light
both does and does not appear real,

it seemed to me that I began
to make out new spirits forming a ring
around the other two circumferences.　　75

Oh true dazzling of the Holy Spirit!
How quick and bright was that light
that my eyes could no longer bear to see!

But Beatrice appeared to me,
so smiling and beautiful that the mind　　80
cannot follow and must leave the vision.

From this I regained my eyes
and raised them to find myself translated
alone with her to a higher realm.

I was aware that I had risen                    85
because the beaming star glowed
redder than ever before. Then

in the language of common
speech, I made my heartfelt offering
to God, as proper to His latest grace.          90

Nor was that sacrifice in my breast
exhausted before I learned my prayer
had been accepted, auspicious,

for splendors appeared to me
in twin rays so bright and fiery that I said,   95
"O Helios! Who emblazons them so!"

And just as distinct with greater
and lesser, the stars flicker between
the world's poles, perplexing wise men

so constellated in Martian depths               100
those rays of light made a hallowed sign
such as quadrants joining a circle make.

Here memory outstrips my art:
for on the cross there flashed Christ—
and no worthy model by which to tell of it.     105

But he who would take up his cross
and follow Him will pardon my omission
seeing white heaven glow with Christ.

From arm to arm, from crown to foot,
lights moved brilliantly dazzling, meeting      110
and crossing each other, moving along

and beyond, light beams sometimes
streaking across the shade that men
artfully devise to defend against the sun.

So on earth one sees the minutiae                    115
of things long, short, straight, curved, some fast
some late, the sight always changing.

And as the lute and harp, whose
many strings combine in harmony, though
individual notes are hard to discern                 120

so from the spread of lights along
the cross arms, a melody captivated me,
although I did not recognize the hymn.

I did know it meant high praise
because I heard "Arise" and "Conquer"                125
as one who hears without comprehending.

Yet I was transported by the sound:
until then there was nothing that had
ever bound me with such sweetness.

Perhaps my word is too forward                       130
since I delayed my joy in those peerless eyes
in which every longing found respite.

But since one can perceive the seals
of beauty strengthen as they ascend
and since I had not there turned to see them         135

he can excuse me, as I excuse
myself, in order to see the truth: that my
joy at those magnificent eyes grew

the higher, as we rose in perfection.

*Note*

35. a modest voice—i.e., of Solomon.

# Canto XV

[Dante meets the soul of his great, great grandfather, Cacciaguida, who tells of his life in Florence and of his death, following Conrad III.]

Good will, in which the love
that always inspires becomes evident
(just as greed shows in the sinful),

   imposed silence on the sweet lyre
and quieted the holy chords that Heaven's         5
right hand made taut or loosened.

How can souls turn a deaf ear
to valid prayer, who urged me to pray
for them and grew hushed in expectation?

   It's just that such a person should         10
mourn forever for loving something that will
not last, at the expense of eternal love.

As a sudden fireball shoots
through tranquil night air, and catches
eyes previously unmoved, a star         15

   shifting from its position, except
the place from which it burst finds
nothing missing, and the flare subsides,

so from the right arm of the cross
a star streaked from the shining constellation         20
there all the way down to the foot,

   nor did that gem swerve from
the track but crossed the radial lines
like fire seen behind alabaster.

Just so did Anchises' shade                     25
start, if we may trust our greatest Muse,
when he caught sight of his son in Elysium.

*«O sanguis meus, o superinfusa*
*gratia Dei, sicut tibi cui*
*bis unquam celi ianua reclusa».*                30

So the light said: I stared at him.
Then turned to the face of my Lady,
stunned whether I looked this way or that.

For her eyes were glowing
with such warmth I thought mine had touched   35
the source of my grace and Paradise.

Then this light which is joy
to hearing and sight, began speaking
of things too deep for my understanding.

It was not as if he chose                       40
to obscure his thought, but necessity made
him surpass the mark mortals have set.

And when the burning bow
of his affection had been released, his speech
bent and met the mark of our intellect.         45

The first thing I came to understand
was, "Blessed be Thou, Three-in-One,
who proclaim such kindness to my seed."

It was followed by, "The lengthy,
dear hunger I felt from reading the mighty      `50
book of unalterable black and white,

you, son, eased, within this flame
from which I speak. I give thanks to her
who gave you wings for soaring flight.

You believe that your thought                    55
flows from Him who is first to me,
as five and six shine forth from one.

Therefore you do not ask me
who I am, nor why I am more joyful
than any other in this joyful crowd.            60

What you believe is true, for great
and small in this life gaze at a mirror where
what they think has already been thought.

But so that the Sacred Love
in which I gaze with perpetual vision, thirsting   65
with sweet desire, may be best fulfilled

let your voice—secure, direct, glad—
plumb your wishes, your keenest desire,
my answer is already decreed."

I turned to Beatrice, who heard me              70
before I spoke and smiled to me as a sign
that strengthened the wings of my desire.

Then I began, "As soon as you saw
the First Equality, both intellect and love
achieved equal weight in each of you,          75

because the sun which lighted
and warmed you operates so impartially
that all comparisons are lacking.

But among mortals, word
and feeling, for reasons that you know,        80
find their pinions otherwise feathered.

As a mortal, I feel the imbalance
and so it is only with my heart that I
can thank you for this paternal welcome.

I do implore you truly, who are                          85
living topaz, precious set gem, to satisfy
my desire to know your name."

   "O leaf of mine, in whom
I delighted waiting for your arrival here,
I was your root," he said by way of preface;            90

   then, "He, you family's namesake,
whose soul has circled the first ledge
of the Purgatorial mountain for more

   than a century, was my son, father
of your grandfather; thus it well behooves             95
you to ease his toil with good works.

   Florence, circled about with ancient
walls, where terce and nones still resound,
was once peaceful, seemly and pure.

   She had no golden chains                             100
or coronet, no ornate gown or girdle
more noteworthy than she who wore it.

   Then there was no father fearing
the birth of a daughter, for neither age
nor dowry veered too much on either side.              105

   No houses were devoid of families,
nor was there a Sardanapalus to show
what can be done in a bedroom.

   Neither had your Uccellatoio
outdone Rome's Montemalo, which                        110
would come to pass in both rise and fall.

   I have seen Bellincione Berti go by
girded with leather and bone, and his wife
turn from her mirror with face unpainted.

And I have seen Nerli and Vecchio                    115
content to wear leather, their women
dealing in flax, at the spindle all day.

So fortunate they are!  Each wife
was certain of her final resting place, none
was deserted in bed because France called.          120

One watched the cradle over
her baby, speaking in that playful idiom
long used by new fathers and mothers;

the other, sitting at the spinning
wheel, would tell the household tales               125
of Trojans, of Fiesole, and of Rome.

A Cincinnatus or Cornelia would
amaze now as much as a Lapo Salterello,
or Cianghella would have then.

In so quiet and beautiful a place,                  130
citizens safely living in communal life,
bonded by faith, this sweet shelter,

Mary, in pains of childbirth, delivered me,
and within your ancient Baptistery I became
a Christian and Cacciaguida.                        135

Moronto and Eliseo were my brothers.
My wife came to me from the Po valley
and brought with her your surname.

I served in the militia of Emperor
Conrad and such was my valor in his eyes           140
that I was later awarded the girdle of a knight.

I followed him against the iniquity
of that law whose believers usurp from you,
because of the shepherd's sin, your rights.

There I was from those grim people          145
delivered from the unruly world, the love
of which degrades so many souls.

From martyrdom I came to this peace.


## Notes

25. Anchises' shade—In the *Aeneid* (VI), Aeneas meets his father in the Elysian Fields.
28–30. *«O sanguis meus, o superinfusa … celi ianua reclusa»*—"O, my blood, O
abounding grace, to whom was Heaven's gate opened twice, as it was to you?"
31. So the light said—Cacciaguida, Dante's great-great grandfather.
48. to my seed—i.e., to Dante.
74. First Equality—i.e., God.
93. the first ledge of the Purgatorial mountain—the ledge of the Proud.
98. terce and nones—mid-morning and mid-afternoon prayers (i.e., 9 a.m. to 3
p.m.).
107. Sardanapalus—King of Assyria 667–626 BC), known for his debaucheries.
109. Uccellatoio—a hill overlooking Florence.
112. Bellincione Berti—a Florentine nobleman.
115. Nerli and Vecchio—Guelph noblemen and Florentine leaders of Cacciaguida's era.
127. Cincinnatus—See Canto VI, 46 (Quintius).
127. Cornelia—Daughter of Scipio Africanus and mother of tribunes and land
reformers the Gracchi.
129. Cianghella—a Florentine woman, lord of Imola.
136. Moronto and Eliseo—noble Ghibellines, exiled from Florence.
140. Emperor Conrad—Most probably Conrad III (1093–1152), crowned in Milan as
Emperor (1128), engaged in the Second Crusade and was defeated at Damascus.
142–143. the iniquity of that law—Islam.

# Canto XVI

[Cacciaguida tells Dante of the noble and distinguished families of Florence, many of whom were in decline by Dante's time.]

Trivial thing, the pride we take
in noble blood that you can make men honor you
here on earth where our affections languish,

yet I will never marvel at it
for even here where appetite is not perverted—          5
in heaven, I say, I gloried in my blood.

Nobility's a mantle that quickly shrinks.
Unless we add to it day by day, time will come
and surround you with snipping shears.

I spoke in that form of "you"          10
that first began to be used among Romans,
but which the people use less often now.

Whereupon Beatrice, who stood
a little apart, smiling, seemed like that one
who coughed when Guinevere first faltered.          15

So I began, "You are my father.
You give me confidence to speak. You lift
me up so that I am more than I am.

So many streams have poured
into my mind, that it makes of itself a joy          20
because it can endure and does not burst.

Tell me, dear original, who
were my ancestors, and which, when you
were a boy, were the years that made history?

Tell me about the sheepfold of St. John,            25
how large, and who the people were
within it worthy of the loftiest seats?"

As the blowing of a wind causes
coals to burst into flame, so I saw the light
shine all the more at my blandishments.            30

And as its beauty grew before my eyes,
so in a sweeter and more gentle voice,
not in our modern idiom, it said to me:

"from that day when 'Ave' was first said
until my mother (now sainted), heavy            35
with child, gave birth to me,

to its own Leo this flaming star
returned five hundred and fifty times, plus
thirty more, to be rekindled beneath its paw.

My ancestors and I were born            40
in the place where, in the annual games,
all the runners reach the farthest ward.

Of my forefathers, suffice to say
that concerning their names and origins
it is better to keep silent than to speak.            45

All those who lived there at that time
who were fit to bear arms between Mars
and the Baptist were a fifth of those now alive.

But the citizens then, now intermingled
with Campi and Certaldo and Fighine            50
were pure down to the meanest artisan.

It would be far better to have
as neighbors those I speak of and let
Galluzzo and Trespiano be your boundaries

than to have them in and withstand                    55
the smell of Augulione's bumpkin and him of Signa
who even now has an eye for swindling,

if that world of degenerates had not
taken a stepmother's role with Caesar but
had been rather as a mother to her son                60

then one who is Florentine, a merchant
and moneylender would be back in Simifonti,
where his grandfather shifted on the streets.

Then Montemurlo would still have counts,
the parish of Acone would have its Cerchi,            65
and the Valdigrieve still the Buondelmonti.

It has always been the case that
in the confusion of peoples lies a source of illness
in cities, just as surfeit of food makes a body sick;

a blind bull plunges more headlong                    70
than a blind lamb; and very often a single sword
cuts better and more completely than five.

If you think about Luni and Urbisaglia,
how they have perished, and how also Chiusi
and Sinigaglia follow them on the way to doom,        75

it should not be too hard to comprehend,
nor too novel, how families are undone
when you consider that even cities have an end.

All the things you possess also possess
their mortality, like you, although in some the length  80
can be hidden, since your own lives are so short.

And as the revolving of the lunar sphere
continually covers and uncovers the shore,
in the same way does Fortune with Florence.

Thus there is no reason to wonder                    85
at what I shall say of the great Florentines
whose fame is concealed in the past.

I saw the Ughi, saw the Cartellini,
Filippi, Greeks, Ormanni, and Alberichi,
illustrious citizens, even in their decline.          90

I also saw, as great as they were
ancient, the dell'Arca with della Sannella,
and the Ardinghi, Soldanieri, and Bostichi.

Near the gate that is presently
weighed down with a new felony, so                    95
weighty that it will sink the ship,

there were the Ravignani, from
whom descended Count Guido, and all who
take their name from the lofty Bellincione.

The della Pressa already knew                         100
how to govern, and Galigaio already
had his hilt and pommel gilded.

The stripe of vair was already strong:
Galli, Sacchetti, Giuocchi, Fifanti, and Baruchi
and those chagrined by the stave affair.              105

The stock from which the Calfucci
were both was already great, the Arrigucci,
the Sizzi had already taken up high seats.

Oh what I behold of those now undone
by their own pride!  How the golden balls             110
shown when Florence flowered in deeds!

Such were the ancestors of those
who, in vacancies in the Holy See, grew
fat by staying put in the consistory court.

That insolent race that plays                                   115
the dragon to all who flee, but the lamb
to any who bare their teeth, or purses,

was already on the make, though
of such base stock that Donato was galled
when his father-in-law made him kin to them.       120

Already Caponsacci had descended
from Fiesole down to the marketplace;
the Guidi and Infangati already good citizens.

I will tell you something incredible
but true: one entered the small circle by means    125
of a gate named after the della Pera.

Each one that bears the baronial
escutcheon whose name and merit alike
are celebrated on St. Thomas' Day

owe their knighthood and privilege                     130
to him, though he who fringes that ensign
now takes up with the cause of the people.

Already there were the Gualterotti
and the Importuni; spared new neighbors,
their borgo would have been quieter place.         135

The house that gave birth to your
sorrow, whose vindictive wrath felled you
and brought your joyous life to an end,

was itself honored and its companions.
O Buondelmonte, you brought such evil when      140
you fled the nuptials to make another's comfort.

Many would be celebrating who are
now sad, if God had drowned you in the Ema
the first time you made for the city.

But it was fitting that Florence                                 145
sacrifice a victim on that mutilated stone
guarding the city, marking the end of peace.

With these people and others like them
I saw a Florence in such grand repose
that she had no occasion to weep.                                150

With these families I beheld such
a just and glorious people, that the lily
on the staff was never reversed, nor

from dissension switched from white to red."


*Notes*

16. You are my father—i.e., progenitor.
25. the sheepfold of St. John—St. John was the patron saint of Florence.
34. when 'Ave' was first said—i.e., at the Annunciation.
37. to its own Leo this flaming star—Mars.
47–48. Mars and the Baptist—i.e., between the statue of Mars on the Ponte Vecchio and the Baptistry of St. John, boundaries of Florence in Dante's time.
50. Campi and Certaldo and Fighine—These locations (in Florence) were out-of-the-way.
54. Galluzzo and Trespiano—outlying villages.
56. Augulione's bumpkin and him of Signa—Baldo d'Aguglione, a Florentine prior of a castle (Auglione) south of Florence who omitted Dante's name in a decree reinstating Florentine exiles and Fazio dei Morubaldini of Signa, a lawyer known as a shyster.
61. then one who is Florentine—It is not clear who Dante has in mind.
62. Simifonti—a town in Valdessa.
64. Montemurlo—a castle sold to Florence in 1254.
65. Acone—a small town near Florence.
65. Cerchi—members of a powerful Florentine family in Dante's ancestral neighborhood.
66. Valdigrieve—a small Tuscan river south of Florence.
66. Buondelmonti—leaders of the Guelphs in Florence, who left the country to reside in Florence in 1135.
73. Luni—ancient city in northern Tuscany, a ruin.
73. Urbisaglia—of Ancona in the Marche: not yet died out.
74. Chiusi—In Val di Chiana, originally an ancient Etruscan site, nearly succumbed to malaria.
75. Sinigaglia—north of Ancona. This coastal city was ravaged by malaria.

88–89. Ughi … Ormanni, and Alberichi—old families of the 11th century.

92. the dell'Arca …Soldanieri, and Bostichi—all powerful families in Cacciaguida's time but either in decline or extinct in Dante's.

97. Ravignani—another of the distinguished Florentine families, although extinct by Dante's time.

98. Count Guido—Guido Guerra was praised in the *Inferno* (XVI), despite being punished among the Sodomites.

99. Bellincione—the great grandfather of Count Guido.

100. The della Pressa—prominent in Cacciaguida's time, elected to govern lands near Florence.

101. Porta San Piero nobility, already knighted ("his hilt and pommel gilded") in Cacciaguida's time.

103. stripe of vair—ermine piping.

104. Galli, Sacchetti, Giuocchi, Fifanti, and Baruchi —Significant Florentine families of Cacciaguida's time.

105. the stave affair—The Florentine Salt Tax Department used the "stave" as unit of measurement, but skewed the measurements, thus skimming the audit.

106. Calfucci—The Calfucci line was collateral with the Donati, of which Gemma, Dante's wife, was a member.

107–108. Arrigucci, the Sizzi—important Florentine families, in Dante's time either extinct (Arrigucci) or in decline (Sizzi).

12–123. Caponsacci…Infangati … Guidi—Ghibelline families in decline.

126. the della Pera: an old Florentine family.

129. St. Thomas' Day—December 21.

131. him—Marquis Hugh of Brandenburg, who came to Florence with emperor Otto III and while there conferred nobility on several Florentine families.

133–135. Gualterotti and the Importuni—leading Guelph families of Cacciaguida's time, by Dante's fallen in stature.

140. Buondelmonti—Buondelmonti dei Buondelmonte, a wealthy young Florentine Guelph engaged in a feud with a Ghibelline knight, Oddo Arrighi, of a Ghibelline family. Oddo demanded satisfaction through marriage to his niece. Buondelmonti broke off the engagement at the last minute because of another woman. On this way to his new wedding, Buondelmonti was murdered by Oddo beneath the statue of Mars on the Ponte Vecchio, an act that shocked Florence and instigated longstanding divisions between the factions.

143. Ema—a small river south of Florence. Buondelmonte, whose family was from the country, would have crossed it to enter Florence.

148. With these people—i.e., the old families.

152–153. the lily on the staff was never reversed—The coming of the Guelphs and the expulsion of the Ghibellines in 1251 meant the reversal of the standard from red lily on a white field.

154. from dissension switched from white to red—Dante suggests the reversal (from white to red) to signify blood.

# Canto XVII

[Dante asks Cassiaguida to tell him about the future, and Cassiaguida complies. However, he reminds Dante that his *Commedia* and the fame that will follow in future generations will be ample compensation for his exile.]

Like him who came to Clymene
to ascertain the truth of what he heard, who
still makes fathers wary of their poor sons,

such was I and such was heard
by Beatrice and by the holy light that first          5
on my account changed its place.

Therefore, my Lady said, "Send
the flame of your desire; let it issue
well imprinted with the inner stamp,

not because your talk increases          10
what we know, but that better you speak
your thirst so that your cup may be filled."

Oh my treasured root, so raised,
that as earthly minds perceive, no triangle
can contain two that are obtuse,          15

you see in contingent things
rather how they are in themselves, the point
at which time becomes timeless.

While I was with Virgil,
on the mountain where souls are repaired          20
and descending into the dead world,

serious words were spoken
of my future life, and yet I feel I am
foursquare against the blows of chance;

and so, my desire would be content                    25
to hear what fortune now approaches
because an expected arrow flies more slowly.

So I spoke to the same light
that had spoken to me before, and as Beatrice
wished, I made my wish my confession.                 30

Not in dark riddles that used to snare
foolish folk before the Lamb of God,
who taketh away sins, was slain,

but in plain and precise words
that loving father, at once hidden, yet                35
revealed by his own smile, replied,

"Contingency, that does not
extend beyond the book of matter,
is depicted whole in the Eternal:

but this implies no necessity,                         40
any more than a ship sailing downstream
is moved by the eyes that mirror it.

Since then, even as to the ear
sweet harmony comes from an organ,
so to my eyes there comes a view                       45

of what time is preparing for you.
As Hippolytus was forced to flee Athens
by a merciless, deceitful mother, so you

must leave Florence. So it
is willed, planned, and shall be done by one           50
scheming where daily Christ is for sale.

As usual, the offended party
will cry out, but the vengeance demanded
of Truth shall yet witness what is true.

You shall abandon everything                                    55
for which you care most deeply; this is
the arrow that the bow of exile shoots first.

You shall know how salty the bread
of others is, and how hard a footpath
takes you up and down another's stairs.                          60

But what will weigh more on your
shoulders will be the evil and foolhardy
company you will fall into in this valley;

all ingrates, all mad, and impious,
they will range against you, but soon                            65
it will be their cheeks, not yours, burning.

Concerning their bestiality, the proof
will be in their actions, while you will do well
for having made a party of one.

Your first refuge and first hostel                               70
will come courtesy of a grand Lombard
whose ladder carries a sacred bird.

And so benign will be his regard for you,
that with the give and take between you,
that will be first that is last to others.                       75

With him beside you, you shall see
one impressed so deeply by his birth star
that his achievements will all be notable.

The people have not yet noticed him
because of his youth, since only nine years                      80
have these wheels turned around him.

But even before Gascon cheats
noble Henry, this one's virtue will sparkle,
having no care for silver nor worry about toil.

His magnificence will be such                                    85
that his enemies will assuredly become
powerless to keep tongues mute.

You may rely on him and his benefits.
The fate of many shall be transformed by him,
mendicant and wealthy changing places.                           90

What I tell you about him inscribe
in the mind—but do not speak it"; and he said
things to those present that were incredible,

then added, "Son, now you see
my account of what was said to you; you see        95
the snares hidden behind just a few years.

Yet bear your neighbors no envy
for your life will have a future that reaches
far beyond their crimes and punishments."

By his silence that blessed soul                                 100
revealed that he had stopped weaving the woof
across the web with the warp I had prepared.

I began as one who doubts
and craves counsel from of a person
who sees, rightly wills, and loves.                              105

"Father, well do I perceive how time
charges toward me to deal me such a blow
as would be crushing to the least prepared.

Therefore, it is well I arm myself
with foresight, for if the dearest place to me be lost,   110
through my poems, I do not lose the others.

Down through the world of endless bitterness
and the mountain, from whose beautiful peak
the eyes of my Lady lifted me. And after,

through heaven from light to light                    115
I have learned things that, if I were to tell them
again, many would taste bitter herbs.

And I am a timid friend to truth,
I am afraid I will lose my life with those who
will come to refer to this as the ancient time."      120

The light in which there smiled
the treasure I had discovered there, began
to flash as a gold mirror would in the sun.

Then it replied, "the conscience
dark with shame for its own or another's acts         125
will indeed find what you say to be blunt.

Nevertheless, shun all falsehood,
make manifest all that you have seen
and let them scratch where it itches.

For your words may be bitter                          130
at first taste, but when digested,
they leave thereafter a vital nutriment.

The cry you raise shall strike,
like the wind, the highest peaks,
and, for honor, that is no slight argument.           135

Thus within these spheres are shown,
on the Mount and down in the dolorous
valley, only the souls known to fame,

because the listener's spirit is restless
and will not have faith or place its trust            140
in things whose root is unknown and obscure

or other argument not made plain."

## Notes

1. him who came to Clymene—Phaeton. Told that Apollo was not his father, Phaeton goes to his mother (Clemene) to find the truth. Apollo meanwhile consents when Phaeton asks to drive the chariot of the sun but is unable to control the horses, threatening the earth. Zeus intervenes with a thunderbolt, killing Phaeton.

47. Hippolytus—Rejecting the advances of his mother Phaedra, Hippolytus is slandered by her and driven out by his father Theseus, who calls on Poseidon for vengeance. Poseidon sends a bull from the sea to destroy Hippolytus (Ovid, *Metamorphoses*, XV).

71. a grand Lombard—his patron in Verona, Can Grande.

82–83. Gascon cheats noble Henry—Henry II, with whom Dante's hopes of returning from exile lay, went to Rome at the invitation of Pope Clement V (Gascon), only to be excommunicated.

# Canto XVIII

[Cacciaguida speaks of God's warriors. Dante and Beatrice rise to the sixth sphere, that of Jupiter, where he witness a string of lights that spell a message about justice. Then the lights arrange themselves into the figure of the Eagle.]

Now the holy mirror delighted
in its own words, and in tasting mine
I tempered the bitter with the sweet.

Then the Lady who guided me said
"Change your thoughts. Remember that I        5
dwell near the One who relieves every hurt."

I turned to the sound of love, of my
comfort, and then what love I met
within those eyes is more than I can tell,

not only fearful my power of speech        10
might fail, but because my mind cannot return
so far above itself unless another guide me.

I can only tell you this: that
whenever I gazed at her, my soul
was freed from every other desire,        15

as the Eternal Delight rayed
directly into Beatrice's face, and then
in its reflection, filled me with joy.

Overwhelming me with the radiance
of her smile, she said to me: "Turn and listen.        20
Paradise is not only in my eyes."

As we see, the look sometimes
reveals the affection, if what the soul
wishes is so strong as to seize it.

So in the flaming of the holy fire                    25
to which I turned, I met the desire
in that light to have further words.

He said, "In this fifth level,
from the tree that lives from its crown,
bears fruit eternally, and never loses leaf,          30

live blessed spirits that below,
before they came to heaven, were of such
renown that they would enrich any Muse.

Now observe the arms of the cross:
each soul I name will flash as quick                  35
as lightning does through a cloud.

I saw a streak of lightning set loose
as the name of Joshua was pronounced,
and the light reached me before the name did.

At the name of the great Maccabee                     40
I saw another light, spinning; the string
that spun that top was its own joy.

Next came Charlemagne and Roland.
I followed these two lights the way
the eye follows a falcon in flight.                   45

Then William of Orange, Renouard,
and the Duke Godfrey led my sight
along the cross, and Robert Guiscard.

The light that had spoken to me
moved away and mingled with the others;               50
I heard his skill, singing in heaven's choir.

I turned to my right to see
from Beatrice what my duty, either
by words or gesture, should be.

I saw her eyes shine with                                    55
such radiance that her countenance
was more beautiful than I had ever seen it.

   And as a man begins to feel
greater joy in doing good day by day,
and begins to see the advance of virtue,                     60

   so I became aware that my circling
together with heaven had increased its arc,
observing that miracle become more lustrous.

   Such a change may be noticed
straightaway in a pale woman's face                          65
when the burden of bashfulness lifts,

   and such I saw when I turned
around, by the whiteness of the temperate
sixth star, which had gathered me to it.

   In the torch of Jupiter, I saw                 70
the shining light of love which was there
and in my eyes marked our language.

   And just as birds flying off
from a riverbank, as if taking joy in their food,
flock in rings or some other shape,                          75

   so it was that in the lights
those blessed creatures circled and sang,
becoming figures: D, then I, then L.

   First they moved rhythmically
to their song, and then, finishing, they formed              80
a letter, then paused and were silent.

   O divine Pegasus, you who give
glory to men and a long life, who also give,
through them, glory to realms and cities,

bestow your light on me that I                                   85
may show these letters, as I conceived them!
May your power show in these brief verses!

Then they took shape: five times
seven vowels and consonants, and I could
make out the parts as they were spelled out.          90

DILIGITE IUSTITIAM were the verb
and noun that came first of those depicted,
then QUI IUDICATIS TERRAM followed.

Then, in the M of the fifth word
they stayed in place; Jupiter seemed to be           95
silver there with a background of gold.

And I saw other lights descend
to the apex of the M and pause there, singing,
I think, of the Good that draws them.

Then, as sparks fly when one                                 100
pokes burning logs (and fools are wont to use
the occasion to engage in fortune-telling),

there seemed to erupt over
a thousand lights, some more, some less,
as apportioned by the sun that lights them;         105

and once each spark eased
into place, I saw that the distinctive fire
represented an eagle's head and neck.

Who paints there has no guide
but guides Himself; from Him comes                      110
the guiding power to build a nest.

The other blessed ones, contented
at first to bloom as a lily on the M,
with slight movement completed the design.

O gentle star, what and how many　　　　115
jewels showed me that earthly justice depends
on heaven where you are bejeweled!

Therefore, I pray the Mind, where
begins your motion and power, to watch
the source of smoke that dims your rays,　　120

so that His wrath again descend
on those would buy and sell in the temple
whose walls were built by signs and martyrs.

O Heavenly soldiers, whom I
contemplate, pray for those gone astray,　　125
by bad example, within their earthly lives.

Though once it was with swords
to war, now war means here and there taking
bread the compassionate Father denies no one.

But you who only write to blot out,　　　130
remember: Peter and Paul, who died
to save the vineyard you trample, still live.

Well may you say, "I, whose desire
is set on the one who lived in solitude
and who, for a dance, was led to martyrdom,　135

do not know the Fisherman or Paul."

## Notes

28. He—i.e., Cacciaguida.

38. Joshua—led the Jews to the Promised Land, following Moses.

40. the great Maccabee—Judas Maccabaeus, Jewish warrior who warred successfully against the Syrians (ca. 160 BC) and weathered attempts to put down the Jewish religion.

43. Charlemagne—drove the Moors from Europe.

43. Roland—nephew and defender of Charlemagne.

46. William of Orange—Count of Orange, was considered the greatest Christian knight; he fought against the Saracens in southern France and is the hero of several medieval romances.

47. Duke Godfrey—leader of the First Crusade (1096) and first Christian king of Jerusalem.

48. Robert Guiscard—Norman warrior fought against the Saracens in Italy (1046). He subsequently became duke of Puglia and Calabria.

63. that miracle—Beatrice.

70. In the torch of Jupiter—the planet Jupiter. Dante is now in the sixth sphere.

78. becoming figures: D, then I, then L.—The first four letters of the Latin below.

91–93. DILIGITE IUSTITIAM...QUI IUDICATIS TERRAM—i.e., love justice, you who are the judges of the earth.

107–108. The distinctive fire represented an eagle's head and neck—The eagle formed by the lights symbolizes God's justice, whereas earlier the eagle represented God's empire (and the Roman standard).

113. as a lily on the M—The "M" of the eagle suggests "Monarchia," so monarchy describes as well the lily, emblem of the French, at first seemingly independent, now merged with the Empire.

# Canto XIX

[The Eagle speaks of God's justice. Dante wonders about God's justice in denying salvation for virtuous pagans. The Eagle denounces a series of corrupt Christian types.]


There now appeared before me
with open wings, a beautiful image
formed by jubilant souls in unison.

Each seemed a ruby in which
a ray of sun was burning so that the light      5
reflected straight into my eyes.

What I have to tell you now
has never been reported by voice, nor
written in ink, nor imagined in fantasy.

I saw move and likewise heard      10
the beak utter with its voice: "I" and "mine,"
when in conception it was "we" and "ours."

It began: "Being just and merciful
I am exalted here to that glory
beyond which desire cannot go.      15

I left my memory on earth
such that the malevolent there commend
it, but do not follow its example.

Just as a sole warmth comes
from many embers, so one sound came      20
from that image, as if from many loves."

And I said, "O perpetual flowers
of eternal joy, that make one fragrance
for me from all your odors, breathe

forth your words that will relieve                                25
me of the fast that has long kept me
hungering, not finding any food on earth."

I know well that God's justice
has its mirror in another realm, that you
do not apprehend it through any veil.                             30

You know how attentively
I listen; you also know the doubt for whose
answer I have hungered for so long.

As the falcon, emerging from
his hood, starts to spread eager wings                           35
and make himself fine with preening,

so moved that standard, made
of grace divine, and from it songs known
to him who dwells there rejoicing.

Then it began, "He who turned His                                40
compass to the world's limits and ordered
what was occult, what revealed, within it,

could not imprint his power
throughout the universe, but that his Word
should not remain in infinite excess.                            45

In proof of this the first proud one,
the paragon of every creature, fell
prematurely, by not waiting for the light.

And so it appears that each
minor nature is a paltry receptacle for that                     50
good, self-measured, and without end.

In consequence, our vision,
which must consist of rays of the Mind
of which all things are replete,

cannot by its own nature be                                55
powerful enough to discern its origin
beyond what is apparent. Therefore

the vision of your world is
no more able to fathom Eternal Justice
than your eye is to penetrate the ocean,                    60

for although near shore, sight
can touch bottom, in open sea: not,
yet the bottom is there, hidden.

There is no light, except
from that clear serene; everything else                     65
is darkness or shadow and poison of flesh.

Now you see opened the place
of living Justice hidden from you,
to which you put so many questions.

For you would say, "Think of a man                          70
born by the Indus: there is no one who
reasons of Christ who can read or write;

and all his impulses and good
acts are, as far as human reason
is concerned, without sin in word or deed.                  75

He dies unbaptized and without faith:
where is the justice in his sentence?
Where is his fault, if he does not believe?

And who are you to sit in judgment
of events a thousand miles away, considering               80
the brief span of your short vision?

For the subtle man, certainly
if there were no Scriptures for guidance,
then there would be grounds for doubt.

O earth-bound animals!  O turbid                    85
minds!  The Primal Will—in itself good—
does not move from Itself, the Supreme Good.

    Only what accords to it is just;
it is swayed by no created good
but, beaming forth, causes good.                    90

    Just as a stork turns around
her nest when she has fed her children,
and those fed look up at her, just so

    did the blessed image turn,
and so did I, while its wings moved,                95
driven by so many wills in concert.

    Circling, it sang and said, "Just as
my singing exceeds your understanding,
so is the Eternal Judgment to you mortals."

    Those flames of the Holy Spirit                100
were stilled, within the sign that made
the Romans revered around the world,

    and it resumed, "Into this realm
no one rose who did not believe in Christ,
neither before nor after he was crucified."        105

    But see how many now cry 'Christ!
Christ!' who at the Judgment will be far less
near to Him than one who never knew him.

    Such Christians will the Ethiopians
condemn when you set apart two companies,          110
the one forever rich, the other poor.

    What will the Persians say
when they shall see that volume opened
in which are written down all their obscenities?

There shall be seen, among Albert's                      115
deeds, one that will set the pen moving, for which
the kingdom of Prague shall be deserted.

There shall be seen the Seine's woe
for that debaser of the coin, who will meet
death suddenly in a wild boar's skin.                     120

There shall be seen the pride inciting
thirst, that makes the Scot and Englishman
so crazed they cannot keep within bounds.

There seen too the effeminate
lechery of the Spaniard and the Bohemian                  125
who never knew valor, nor wished to know.

There be seen the Cripple of Jerusalem
marked by an 'I' for his goodness,
and for the reverse, marked by an 'M.'

Seen the cowardice and greed                              130
of him who guards the Island of Fire
where Anchises ended his long life,

and to show how trivial it is
his record will be tightened and abbreviated
to indicate smallness in a small space.                   135

And it will be clear to all
the sordid deeds of uncle and brother,
who each dishonored a nation and crown.

And there shall be seen the Kings
of Norway and Portugal and Rascia's whose                 140
evil was he counterfeited Venice's coin.

O happy Hungary, if she let herself
escape abuse! And Navarre, if her mountain
ring could serve as a shield! In consequence

of this, may everyone regard Nicosia                     145
and Famagusta, whose people moan and wail
for their own small beast, that manages

to keep pace from the other side.


*Notes*

1–2. There now appeared before me with open wings, a beautiful image—The
eagle composed of the souls of the just and temperate rulers, the symbol of
divine justice.

46. the first proud one—i.e., Lucifer.

109. the Ethiopians—i.e., pagans.

112. the Persians—i.e., pagans.

115. Albert's—Albert I of Austria, who invaded in 1304.

118. the Seine's woe ... a wild boar's skin—Philip IV ("the Fair" 1268–1304),
disastrously devalued the French currency and died when a wild boar ran
under his horse.

121–122. Scot and Englishman—notorious for endlessly skirmishing.

125. the Spaniard and the Bohemian—Ferdinand IV of Castile (1285–1312)
and Leon Wenceslas of Bohemia (1230–1253).

127. the Cripple of Jerusalem—Charles II of Naples (1254–1309), titular king
of Jerusalem. So-called because of lameness.

131. him who guards the Island of Fire—Frederick II (1194–1250), Holy
Roman Emperor and King of Sicily ("the Island of fire").

132. Anchises—Father of Aeneas.

139–140. Kings of Norway and Portugal—Haakon V Magnusson (1270–1319)
and Dionysus (1279–1325), also called Diniz.

140–141. Rascia's whose evil was he counterfeited Venice's coin—Orosius II of
Rascia (modern day Serbia) counterfeited the coinage of Venice (ca. 1287).

142. happy Hungary—Charles Martel of Anjou's throne was usurped by
Andrew III.

143. Navarre—Joanna of Navarre (wife of French King Philip the Fair) is
meant here, the "ring" being the Pyrenees protecting Navarre from France.
Though she was ruler of Navarre, on her death it was annexed by France.

145–146. Nicosia and Famagusta—cities of Crete. "[T]heir own small beast":
Henry II, one of the debauched kings of Christendom, here diminished in
stature.

# Canto XX

[The Eagle explains which souls compose its eye. These include Trajan and Ripheus, surprising Dante, who wants to know how pagans can be in Heaven. The Eagle explains and concludes that God's knowledge exceeds our comprehension.]

When He who illuminates all the world
descends so far below our hemisphere
that day is consumed on every side,

the heavens, lit by sun alone,
suddenly shows itself again, with many         5
lights reflecting the resplendent one;

so this celestial change came
to mind, when in the blessed beak, the sign
of the world and its leaders fell silent

because those living lights were now         10
shining brighter, as they began their songs,
to my memory now transient and fading.

O sweet love that mantles you
in smiles, how keen the sound of your flutes
played only with the breath of holy thought.         15

When those precious, brilliant jewels
with which the sixth light shone
imposed silence on their angelic ringing,

I seemed to hear a river murmuring,
clear, that descends from stone to stone,         20
showing the fullness of its mountain.

And as sound forms
on a harp's neck and even as the wind
that penetrates the hole of a pipe,

so it was without delay 25
that the eagle's murmur began to rise
up inside its neck as if it were hollow

and became a voice there,
through the beak and in the form of words
to my waiting heart, where I inscribed them. 30

"The part in me that sees and endures
the sun, as mortal eagles do, I want you
now to fix your gaze there," it said,

"because of the fires that form
my shape, the ones by which my eye 35
sparkles in my head are highest.

That one who shines as pupil
was the singer of the Holy Spirit,
who carried the ark from town to town:

he knows the worth of his song 40
as the effect of his own counsel,
and his bliss is commensurate to it.

Of the five who form my brow
the one closest to my beak was he
who consoled the poor widow for her son; 45

now he knows by experiencing
the sweet life and its opposite, how dear
the cost is of not following Christ.

And he who comes next,
highest, in the arc of which I speak, 50
postponed his death through penitence;

now he has learned that judgment
is unchanging, though worthy prayer can
delay today's events until tomorrow.

The next went to Greece with the laws          55
and me, ceding place to the Shepherd—
his good intentions bore bad fruit;

now he knows that the evil
from his good deeds will not harm his soul,
though the world were thereby destroyed.          60

The one you see on the downward arc
was William, and the land that mourned his death
now mourns the life of Charles and Frederick;

now he knows how heaven
loves a just king, as he makes this known          65
by the radiance of his being;

who would believe down
in the errant world that the Trojan Riphea was
fifth among the holy lights in this round?

And now he knows well the world          70
cannot see Divine Grace: even his
sight cannot discern the bottom.

Like a lark that ranges through
the air, at first singing, then falling silent,
satisfied with its last sweet notes          75

so the emblem seemed to me
the image of eternal pleasure, by whose
will all things become what they are.

*Regnum caelorum* endures violence
from ardent love and living hope: these only          80
can defeat God's will, but not as one man

conquers another. Rather it conquers
because it is conquered, and, conquered,
conquers through its own goodness.

The first and fifth among the living                85
souls making up my eyebrow astonished
you, as you beheld the angel's realm.

They departed their bodies, not
as you think, pagans, but as firm Christians:
one grieved in the pierced feet and one would.        90

One rose from Hell—from which
no one may return—to flesh and bones,
and this was reward for living hope,

the living hope that strengthened
his prayers to God to resuscitate him               95
and make it possible for him to find his will.

This glorious soul, returning to flesh
where it lived so briefly, believed in Him
who could do him such a service,

and believing, was kindled to such fire            100
by the true love that when he died a second time
he was deigned worthy to join our festivity.

The other soul, by grace welling
up from a source so deep that no eye
of any creature can reach the bottom,              105

put all his love on righteousness,
and God, with grace on grace, opened
his eyes to our future redemption;

he believed it, and from that day
forward he would no longer suffer the stink        110
of paganism, and he censured the perverse.

He was baptized more than a thousand
years before baptism was, and those three women
you saw at the right wheel were there for him.

O predestination, how remote                    115
your root is from those who cannot see
the Primal Cause in its entirety!

And you, mortal, show restraint
in judging, for we who see God now
do not yet know who all the elect are.          120

And yet such a lack is sweet,
because our good lies in this perfect good
for whatever God wills, we also will."

So with that divine image
a sweet medicine was given to me               125
to correct my short-sightedness.

And as a good lute player lends
his chords' vibrations to a good singer,
making the song all the more pleasant,

so, as the eagle spoke, I can                   130
remember the two holy lights, two souls,
as if they blinked their eyes in time, their flames

moving in accord with the words.

## Notes

31–32. The part in me that sees and endures the sun—See note to Canto I, 50.

37. That one—i.e., King David.

44–45. Of the five… the one closest to my beak—Emperor Trajan (57–117 AD). Dante, following Aquinas, saw in Trajan the example of a virtuous pagan. Trajan also appears in *Purgatorio* (X, 70–90), where he offers justice to a poor woman. Long in Limbo, he is taken up into Heaven.

49. And he who comes next—Hezekiah's deathbed repentance led to fifteen more years of life (II Kings xx).

55. The next went to Greece—Emperor Constantine (c. 272–337 AD) took the empire to Greece, ceding the western part to Church in Rome (the Shepherd).

62. William—William the Good (William II), King of the Two Sicilies (1166–89).

63. Charles and Frederick—Charles the Lame and Frederick II, who succeeded William.

68. Trojan Riphea—The *Aeneid* mentions Riphea as the most just of the Trojans (*Aeneid* II).

79. Regnum *caelorum*—the Kingdom of Heaven.

89. one grieved in the pierced feet—Trajan, who lived during the time of Christ.

89. one would—The just Trojan Ripheus who believed in the future crucifixion, having been granted a vision. Hence his placement in Heaven.

91. One rose from Hell—Trajan.

94. the living hope—Gregory I, who prayed for Trajan's salvation.

104. The other soul—i.e., Ripheus.

113. those three women—the Three Theological Virtues.

# Canto XXI

[Dante and Beatrice rise to the seventh sphere, that of Saturn. Here Dante encounters a celestial ladder and meets the souls of the contemplatives. The soul of Peter Damian comes forth and explains the nature of predestination, then turns to Papal corruption.]

    Already my eyes were fixed on the face
of my lady, and my mind with them,
and all other purpose was dimmed.

    But she did not smile; rather began:
"if I were to smile, you would be like Semele      5
when she was blasted, because

    my beauty, as it ascends the stairs
of the eternal palace, burns brighter,
as you know, the higher we climb,

    and were it not tempered, its      10
very brilliance would strike your eye
the way a lightning bolt splits a branch.

    We have now risen to the seventh
splendor, that, under the burning breast
of a lion, radiates its power downward.      15

    Fix your mind in the direction
of your eyes and make a mirror to reflect
the figure that this mirror will show to you."

    If it were possible to understand
the blessed pasture in her face that my eyes      20
found before they turned to another care,

    then one could see how grateful
and obedient I was to my celestial escort,
balancing joy, this side with that.

Within the crystal that circles 25
the world bearing the name of its dear leader
under whose rule all evil lay dead,

I saw the gold in a sun-struck
beam, and I saw there a ladder lifted up
so high that my sight could not follow it. 30

I also saw so many splendors
descend that I thought every light in the sky
had shot downward, so widespread was it.

As crows instinctively flock
at dawn to warm their chilly feathers 35
in flight, so some fly off without returning,

while others come to the spot
where they started, and yet others sojourn
by wheeling overhead in the same locale,

so it seemed to me such an instinct 40
drove those lights, as they came together,
once they had reached a certain rung.

The light that stopped nearest us
brightened so that I said to myself: I see
well the love you show me. Yet she 45

who teaches me when and how
to speak and when to be silent, pauses, so I,
though wishing otherwise, do well not to ask.

Then she who saw my silence
in the sight of Him who sees all, said 50
to me: "Let loose your deepest desire."

And I began, "I am not worthy
to receive your answer, but for the sake
of one who gave me permission to speak,

you who are blessed to be                                    55
sequestered in joy, do tell me why
you have drawn so near my side.

    And why is it that in this wheel
the sweet symphony of Paradise is silent,
while below sounds with such devotion?"      60

    "Your hearing is as mortal as your sight,"
he replied. "There is no singing here
for the same reason Beatrice has no smile.

    It was only to welcome you
with words and the light that mantles me      65
that I descended the holy stairs.

    Nor was it greater love prompted me;
much and more love blazes above,
as these burning souls make clear to you.

    But the high charity that makes us          70
ready to serve the world's Judge
apportions our tasks, as you observe here.

    "O sacred lamp," I said, "I see indeed
how in this court love is sufficiently free
to follow the eternal Providence;             75

    but what seems hard to comprehend
is why you only were predestined to assume
this office from among your companions."

    I had not come to the last word
when like a rapid millstone that light began  80
turning around its luminous center;

    and the love there answered,
"Divine Light is directed on me and reaches
through the light in which I am manifest,

whose virtue joins my vision                                    85
and lifts me far above myself so that I see
the supreme essence from which it comes.

In this way my flame derives
the joy that makes me burn; my sight
matches the clarity of my flame.                                90

But even the purest soul in heaven,
the seraph whose eye is fixed on God,
cannot satisfy this demand of yours.

The truth you seek lies so deep
in the abyss of Eternal Law, that it is cut                     95
off from the vision of all created beings.

And when you return to the world
of mortals, report this, that they may not
presume to set their feet down such a path.

The mind that shines here                                       100
is murky on earth: how can it do there
what it cannot do when raised to heaven?"

His words so proscribed my
questioning that I let it be and shrank,
humbly, only to ask who he was.                                 105

"Between the coasts of Italy
and not far from your birthplace rise mountains
so lofty that thunder sounds from far below

and these form a ridge where
farther down an hermitage stands, once                          110
dedicated only to the worship of God."

So he began his third speech to me;
and he continued, "it was there that
I grew steadfast in serving God

and lived on plain fare in olive oil,                          115
lightly enduring both heat and cold,
content to live in contemplation.

That cloister used to render souls
abundantly to heaven; now it is empty,
and the cause must soon be revealed.                           120

There I was known as Peter Damian
and became Peter the Sinner when I served
the House of Our Lady on the Adriatic shore.

Little of mortal life was left when
I was called and dragged forth to wear                         125
the Hat that passes from bad to worse.

Cephas came, and the great Vessel
of the Holy Spirit, barefooted and poor,
accepting the chance provision of any host.

But now the priests are so stout,                              130
so hulking, they need assistance on either side,
plus one to lead and one to hold their trains.

They cover their palfreys in their cloaks
so that two animals go under one skin:
O patience! You who must endure such excess!"                  135

At this voice I saw many flames
circling down from grade to grade
and every turn made them more beautiful.

They gathered around him and stopped,
raising a cry so loud that its likeness could not              140
be found here, not did I understand their words

so overcome was I by the thunder.

## Notes

5. Semele—Impregnated with Dionysus by Zeus. she asked to see the god in his glory, and despite his warning, he relented and showed himself, destroying her.

15. a lion—the constellation Leo.

62. he—Peter Damian (c. 1007–c. 1072), Benedictine monk and Cardinal, known for his asceticism.

126. the Hat—i.e., the hat of the Cardinal.

127. Cephas—the name Christ gave to Simon. His new name is the Aramaic for Petrus ("rock").

# Canto XXII

[Dante meets St. Benedict, who explains the Golden Ladder and laments that
so few monks are willing to seek its ascent, being fettered to the world.
Dante and Beatrice then ascend to the eighth sphere, the sphere of the fixed
stars. Beatrice directs Dante's attention to the vastness of their journey so far.]

Stunned with wonder, I turned
to my guide like a child who always
runs back to his most trusted place,

and she, like a mother quick
to help her pallid, panting son                                    5
with her familiar, soothing voice, said,

"Don't you know you are in heaven?
And don't you know that all is holy here,
that every act here issues from pure zeal?

Imagine, since this cry has                                        10
troubled you so, how it would have been
if I had smiled, if they had sung.

If you had grasped the prayer
in their cry, you would already have known
the vengeance you will witness before you die.     15

The heavenly sword cuts
neither in haste, not too slowly, except
to him who waits in dread or desire.

But turn now towards the others,
if you let my words direct your sight,                        20
you will see many remarkable souls.

As she directed me, my eyes turned
and saw a hundred little globes shining,
all the more embellished with mutual rays.

I stood like a person who                                    25
stifles his own longing and does
not question, for fear of seeming rude.

Then the largest and brightest
of those pearls came forward to satisfy
my silent desire to know who he was.                         30

I heard within it, "If you saw
the love that burns in us, you would
have expressed your yearnings.

But because your waiting may
delay your high goal, I will answer                          35
what you were reluctant to ask.

Where Cassino lies on that mountain
there once lived deluded inhabitants
at the summit who revered false beliefs,

I was the first to carry the name                            40
of Him who brought to earth the truth
that transports us upward.

Such lavish grace beamed
down on me that I retrieved souls
from the impiety that had seduced the world.                 45

These other fires were all
contemplatives, men warmed with the heat
that gives birth to holy flowers and fruits.

Here is Macarius, and here, Romualdus,
my brethren whose footsteps remained                         50
bounded in cloisters, their hearts steadfast."

And I to him: "The affection you
have shown in talking to me, and the good
will I behold in all your burning lights

have widened my confidence                                    55
just as the sun expands the rose so that
it can reach the utmost of its blossoming.

Therefore, I pray you, father,
afford me so much grace that I may see,
unveiled, the image of your face."                            60

And he: "Your high wish will
be fulfilled in the last sphere, as will
the desires of the others and my own.

There every wish is perfect,
ripe and whole, in that place is each                         65
part where it has always been

because it is not in space
and has no poles; our ladder reaches
up to it and so surpasses sight.

Infinitely upward, the patriarch                              70
Jacob saw the ladder reach the summit,
when he dreamed it teeming with angels.

But now no one would lift his feet
to the ladder's rung, and my Rule
is so much wasted parchment.                                  75

The walls of the Abbey are caves
now, and the abbots' cowls are sacks
that bulge with moldering wheat.

But even usury does not offend
God as much as the fruit that drives                          80
the hearts of monks so insane.

For whatever the Church has
in its keeping belongs to folk who ask
in God's name, not for monks' kin or worse.

Mortal flesh is so weak down there                    85
that good beginnings last no longer
than a new oak's bearing an acorn.

Peter began with neither gold
nor silver, and I with prayer and fasting,
while Francis found humility in his cloister;          90

if you look at the beginning of each
and regard how each course was spent,
you will behold how white dims to brown.

Yet Jordan's reversed flow and the sea's
parting at God's will were more wonderful             95
to behold than if God now helped his church."

So he said to me, then withdrew
to his company, which closed in on itself,
then like a whirlwind was swept up.

Behind me, the sweet Lady                             100
moved me up the ladder by a single sign,
so did her virtue prevail over my nature.

And never down here, where
nature's laws govern our rising and falling,
was there a flight so swift as my wing's.             105

If I ever return, dear reader,
to that devout triumph for which I cry out
and beat my breast for my transgressions,

you could no sooner have pulled
your finger from a flame and thrust it in again,      110
than I saw, and was in, the sign following Taurus.

O glorious stars, O light pregnant
with virtue, whatever my genius may be,
whatever it acknowledges, you are its source.

When I first felt the Tuscan air, there                      115
rose with you, and with you was hidden, him
who is the father of all mortal life.

And then, when grace was freely
given me to enter the high wheel that turns
you, I was assigned to your region.                          120

My soul sighs devoutly to you now,
to give it strength enough for the stage—
the most difficult—that comes next.

"You are so close to the ultimate
blessedness," Beatrice began, "that you                      125
will have to possess sharp, unclouded vision;

so before entering further here,
look down and consider what a world
I have already put beneath your feet,

so that your heart in joyful fullness                        130
may greet this Triumphant host, whom
it pleases to come through the ethereal round.

My eyes returned from all
the seven spheres and then saw our globe
so that I smiled at its feeble image.                        135

I approve the one who judges
that the least, and who turns his thoughts
elsewhere, may truly be called wise.

I saw Latona's daughter shining
without that shadow that I once thought                      140
the cause of her density and rareness.

Here I could keep, Hyperion,
the vision of your son, and I saw near him
Maia and Dione in their motions.

Then there was Jupiter, moderating                    145
between his son and father, and it was
clear how they varied in their motions.

And all seven made evident
to me their magnitudes, their speeds,
and their distances from each other.                    150

That threshing floor that incites
our savagery, I saw from hills to deltas
all while I turned with the Eternal Twins,

then I turned my eyes again to beauty's eyes.

*Notes*

28–29. Then the largest and brightest of those pearls—St. Benedict (480–ca.
543). Author of the Rule of St. Benedict for monastic life, comprised of two
kinds of rule: spiritual (how to live a Christ-centered life on earth) and
functional (how to run a monastery). His influence in the Middle Ages led to
the rise of monasticism.
37. Cassino—Having fled Rome and its sinfulness, Benedict and his
followers moved in 525 to Monte Cassino and built a monastery there, first
destroying a shrine to Apollo.
49. Macarius—a desert father. Dante may have conflated two historical
persons, both disciples of St. Anthony.
49. Romualdus (956–1027)—founder of the Camaldolese Order, an
offshoot of the Benedictines.
71. Jacob saw the ladder. The ladder of which Jacob dreams is recorded in
Genesis 28, 10–19.
111. the sign following Taurus—i.e., Gemini.
139. Latona's daughter—i.e., the moon.
144. Maia and Dione—i.e., Mercury and Venus.

# Canto XXIII

[At the sun's zenith, Dante is presented Christ in triumph but the vision is too bright to see, and he faints. Beatrice tells Dante to concentrate on the garden: the Rose (Mary) and the lilies (the Apostles). The angel Gabriel greets Mary with a crown of lights, and Dante sees St. Peter.]

Just as a bird in the leaves she loves
who roosts all through the concealing
night on her sweet brood,

eager to behold their looks
and in serious but pleasing labor                    5
to find food for them, waits

yearning on an open branch
and peers out with a fixed look
while the dawn is being born,

so my Lady drew up to her full height               10
and stood at attention to that part
of heaven where the sun seems slowed.

Then I watched her in longing there,
and I became like one who, wishing for more
than he has, must be appeased in hoping.             15

But there was little distance between
the when of waiting and the when of seeing,
as heaven brightened more and more.

And Beatrice said, "See the hosts
of Christ in triumph and all the fruits              20
harvested from the turning of the spheres!"

I saw her face ablaze with light
and her eyes so full of ecstasy that
I must pass on without more account.

Like Trivia at full moon on a cloudless                      25
night, smiling among eternal nymphs
who make every part of the sky filigreed,

I saw above the thousand lights
the sun that illumines all of them, as the sun
lights the heavens in earth's range;                         30

and through that living light I saw
a glowing substance so bright and clear
that my eyes could not sustain their gaze.

O Beatrice!  Dear, sweet guide!
She said: "What overwhelms you now                           35
is a virtue that nothing can oppose.

There is wisdom and strength
in it that opened the road, so long
yearned for, between heaven and earth."

As lightning breaks from a cloud                             40
exploding so that nothing contains it,
and, contrary to its nature, plummets to earth,

so my mind expanded at this feast
until it set off from itself, and what
became of it, it can no longer remember.                     45

"Open your eyes and look straight
at me: you have seen such things
that now you can withstand my smile."

And like one who, waking, has
forgotten his dream and now tries in vain                    50
to retrieve the vision and restore it to memory,

I heard the offering, worthy
of my deepest gratitude, that can never
fade from the book that records the past.

If all the languages that Polyhymnia                    55
and all her sisters, thickened with sweetest
milk, were to come to my help, my song

of the sacred smile illuminating
Beatrice's look would not reach the truth,
not even to the thousandth part.                        60

And so, in rendering Paradise
in my sacred poem, I must make a leap
like a man who finds his way cut short.

Who thinks on such a ponderous
theme and the mortal who shoulders it                   65
will not blame me, if I tremble.

This sea-cleaving prow that
crosses a long and difficult sea, is not for
a little boat, nor for a hesitant pilot.

"Why so enamored of my face                             70
that you do not turn to the beautiful garden
that blossoms under Christ's radiance?

There is the Rose in which the Word
became incarnate; there are the lilies
whose fragrance marks the good way."                    75

Thus Beatrice, and I, now that her
advice made everything ready, once more
 raised my feeble brows to battle.

Standing in shadow I have seen
sunlight stream through a broken cloud                  80
and light up a meadow of flowers.

Just so I saw troops of splendors
lit from above by fiery rays, though
I could not see the source of light.

O kind Power that marks them                    85
with such light, you rose on high
so that my strengthless eyes might see.

The name of that beautiful flower
I have always invoked, morning and evening,
won my soul to look upon a greater fire.       90

And when in both my eyes were shown
the nature and power of that living star
that triumphs there as it does here,

a torch descended from the sky
formed ring-like in a crown                     95
or cincture that whirled around her.

Whatever melody sounds sweetest
on earth and draws the soul most to itself
would sound like a cloud-splitting thunder clap

compared to the sound of that lyre             100
coming in waves from the beautiful sapphire
that crowns brightest heaven's sphere.

"I am angelic love encircling
the sublime joy that breathed our Desire
out from the hostel of the womb,               105

so I will circle you, Lady of Heaven,
until you follow your Son to the utmost sphere
and entering it, make it even more divine."

So the circling melody sealed itself,
and all the other lights within the sphere     110
resounded with the name of Mary.

The royal mantle that spreads across
all the turning spheres and that burns
nearest the breath and laws of God

turned its inner border at such                          115
a distance above us that where
I was it had not yet appeared,

    and so my eyes had no power
to follow the crown of flame that arose
following her Son. And as an infant,                     120

    after suckling, will reach out
its arms to its mother, and as the soul
extends its love into outward flame,

    so I saw each of those lights stretch
its flame upward, and in this way their deep             125
affection for Mary was made clear to me.

    They remained there in sight, singing
"Queen of Heaven" so sweetly that
the delight of it will never leave me.

    Oh how much exuberance is                            130
gathered in those storehouses for those
below who sowed good in the world!

    Here they truly live on the treasure
laid up while they wept in the Babylonian
exile where their gold was left                          135

    and here, victorious, under the Son,
God, and Mary and those of the ancient
covenant and the new, prevails

    the one who holds the keys of glory.

*Notes*

25. Trivia—the moon (i.e., Diana).
55. Polyhymnia—muse of sacred poetry.
73. the Rose—i.e., Mary, the "Mystic Rose."
103. I am angelic love—the Archangel Gabriel, whose Annunciation tells
Mary and the world of the Incarnation.
139. the one who holds the keys—St. Peter.

# Canto XXIV

[The souls dance joyously, and St. Peter comes forth. Beatrice asks him to test Dante's faith. Dante's answers earn him Peter's approbation.]

"O you company chosen for the great
supper of the Blessed Lamb, who feeds you
so that your desire is always fulfilled,

if by the Grace of God this man should
have a foretaste of what falls from your table          5
before time prescribes his death, turn

your mind to his immense longing
and quench him a little, you who drink
forever from that source his thought seeks."

Thus Beatrice; and those souls began          10
turning in circles around fixed poles
and streaked by as if comets.

And as with clocks, when the large
wheel revolves slowly, seemingly still, while
the smaller one, by contrast, flies,          15

so those wheeling dancers, stepping
differently, now fast, now slow, revealed
to me the measure of their riches.

From the sphere I registered most
beautiful, I saw a fire come forth so          20
radiant that it outshone all the others.

That flame turned around Beatrice
three times singing such a divine song
that my imagination can't repeat it.

My pen skips, and I don't write:                    25
the imagination, to say nothing of talk,
cannot paint such bright folds.

O my holy sister, so devoted
in prayer, the love that burns in you
draws me forth from that beautiful sphere.          30

At that point, having stopped,
the blessed fire directed its breath toward
my Lady, and this I have set down exactly.

And she: "O eternal light of that
great one whom our Lord brought down              35
and left the keys to this miraculous joy,

test this man on points mild
or grave, as you will, about the faith
by which you walked on the sea.

If he truly has love, hope and faith,               40
it will not be hidden because you see
where everything appears as it really is.

But since this realm was made
by citizens of the True Faith, it is right
that he should glorify it by speaking of it."       45

And just as a bachelor arms himself
and does not speak until the master sets
the question to examine, not to solve,

so while she spoke I armed
myself with arguments, preparing to meet           50
such a questioner and profession.

"Speak, good Christian, show
your worth: Faith? What is it?" I raised
my brows to the light that breathed this.

Then I turned to Beatrice, and her                55
look prompted me to pour forth
the waters from the depth of my soul.

So I: "May the Grace that gives
me power to confess to the Great Centurion
make my thoughts well expressed."               60

And more: "As the truthful pen
of your dear brother wrote, Father, who, with
you, put Rome onto the path of righteousness,

Faith is the substance of hoped-for
things and evidence of things unseen:            65
this appears to me to be its essence."

Then I heard, "You understand correctly,
if you understand that he put faith first
as substance, and then as evidence."

And I: "The deep things I attest                 70
to here in their appearance are hidden
to my eyes down below and their being

there lies in belief alone,
and belief is founded on high hope
and takes on the nature of a substance.          75

From this belief we reason
with syllogisms, being unable to see more;
thus by nature it partakes of argument."

And then I heard: "If everything
we learned below were understood so well         80
there would be no room for the sophist."

The burning love breathed these words,
then added, "Now this coin is appraised;
we know its composition and weight.

But tell me if you have it in your bag.          85
Then I: "Yes, it's so round and shining,
nothing in its minting leaves me in doubt."

Then from its bright depths there
issued a light that said, "This precious jewel
on which all other virtues are founded:          90

how did you happen to acquire it?
I answered, "The great stream pouring
from the Holy Spirit on ancient and new

reasons so conclusively that all
other demonstration seems at once,          95
by comparison, obtuse to me."

Then I heard, "The ancient and new
propositions that are so conclusive to you—
how do you know they are divine?"

And I: "The proof to me comes          100
in the works that followed, for nature
cannot forge such iron on its anvil."

Then the reply, "Who assures you that
these truths are real? Whatever presents itself
as proof still needs to prove itself, not others."          105

If the world turned to Christianity,"
I said, "without miracles, then that would be
a miracle a hundred times greater than any.

For you entered poor and starving
in the field to sow the good plant that was          110
a vine once, but has now become a thorn."

When this was finished, the spheres
resounded with "*Te Deum Laudamus*," sung
in a melody heard only there above.

And that Baron, who had already                    115
led me from branch to branch in examination
as we were approaching the last leaves

recommenced, "By the Grace whose
love speaks with your mind—and until now
as it should, through your open mouth—            120

I do approve of what has emerged.
But now you must express what you believe
and then say the source of your faith."

And I say, "I believe in One God,
everlasting, who moves all the worlds, though     125
He is motionless, through love and desire.

And for such faith not only do I
have proofs both physical and metaphysical,
but also the truth that rains down on that place

through Moses, the Prophets, the Psalms,          130
through the Gospel, and through you, who wrote
when you were sanctified by the Holy Spirit.

And I believe in three Eternal
Persons, and these I believe one essence,
hence one and triune, both "is" and "are."        135

The deep and divine conditions
I touch upon here have often stamped
my mind with the evangelical doctrine.

This is the principle, the spark
that grows into a living flame and then,          140
like a star in heaven, the light is in me.

Then, like a lord who approves of
what he hears from a servant and grateful
for the good news, embraces him,

the apostolic light at whose command          145
I had spoken when formerly silent, sang
benedictions and encircled me three times,

such was his delight in my speaking.


*Notes*

34–35. And she: "O eternal light of that great one—Beatrice is addressing Peter.

59. Great Centurion—St. Peter, chief soldier in Christ's militia.

62. your dear brother—St. Paul.

113. De Deum Laudamus—We praise Thee, Lord.

115. that Baron—i.e., St. Peter.

# Canto XXV

[St. John blesses Dante, but Beatrice entreats St. James (the Apostle of Hope) to examine Dante on the subject. With Dante's success in answering James, St. John appears, and Dante is blinded by the radiance of Love.]

If ever this sacred poem to which
both heaven and earth have set their hand
and the many years of labor that left me lean

   wins over the cruelty of those who
banished me from that pretty sheepfold where      5
I slept as a lamb, opposed to the warring wolves,

   I will return a poet in a different voice,
with matured fleece, and at the source
of my baptism, put on the laurel crown.

   It was there I acquired the faith      10
that counts souls for God, and then
for that faith Peter crowned my brow.

   Then a light moved toward us
from that sphere where, from Christ's
vicarage on earth, appeared the first fruit.      15

   And my Lady, filled with joy, said,
"Look! Look there! You can see below
the Baron who draws souls to Galicia."

   As when a dove draws near
its companion, and begins to circle      20
and coo to make a show of its affection

   so I beheld those grand and glorious
princes in mutual greeting, giving praise
for the feast served in heaven.

But when they were done with                          25
their salutations, they stopped and stood
before me, in silence, and too bright to see.

   Then Beatrice said, smiling,
"Renowned life, by whom the largesse
of our court has been described,                      30

   let hope go forth at this heavenly height:
you can, because you figured as symbol
when Jesus gave more light to his three."

   "So, raise your head and rest assured
that whatever comes here from the mortal              35
world must first mature in our radiance."

   This comforting saying came from
the second flame, and I raised my eyes
to the hills, until then lowered by such brilliance.

   "Because from His grace our Emperor                40
has willed that, before death, you will face
his Counts in His most inner hall, that

   having seen the truth of this court, you
may, in yourself and others, strengthen hope
that makes men love the good down on earth;          45

   now say what hope is, how much it
quickens the mind, and where it comes from."
So spoke the second flame a second time.

   And that pious one who guided
my wings' pinions on such a soaring flight            50
anticipated what I was about to say—

   "There is no Church Militant child
with more hope, as you can make out
in the Sun that shines on all our band.

And that is the reason he was allowed            55
to come from Egypt to see Jerusalem
before the end of his martial days.

The two other points you have raised,
not for your sake, but that he may report
below how much of this hope is pleasing,            60

I leave to him; he will not find
them difficult or arrogant. So let him
answer—and God's grace help him!"

As a student ready and willing
in his newfound expertise to answer            65
his master and thus to show off his learning,

I said, "Hope is the certain expectation
of distant glory; it is the result
of divine grace and of merit achieved.

This light came by way of many            70
stars, but it was instilled first in my heart
by the greatest singer to the greatest Lord.

He sang, 'Let those who know
Your name put their hope in you.'
Who can have my faith and not know it?            75

You instilled me with your Epistle
like dew, just as he did, and I am full
and ready to rain down, in turn, on others."

While I was saying this, in the live
breast of that light there flashed a flame            80
as insistently and quick as lightning.

It sighed, "love that makes me
burn for the virtue that followed me
to the palm and from the field of battle,

wills me to breathe to you, who delight        85
in this virtue, and I should be grateful
for words telling what hope has promised."

And I: "The Old and New Testaments
set the goal—and this shows it to me—
for those God has made his friends.        90

Isaiah says that in his own land,
each shall be dressed in double garments,
and his land is this very sweet life.

And your brother, too, when
he writes about the white robes, makes        95
this revelation clearly manifest to us."

When I had finished speaking,
I heard, "*Sperent in te!*" ring out over me,
to which all the spheres made a response.

And then one soul among them became        100
so bright that had the Crab such a star,
a winter month would be one day long.

And just as a happy maiden rises
and goes to join a dance honoring the bride,
with no thought of drawing attention to herself,   105

so I beheld that splendor brighten
and fly to the two flames that whirled
in a ring to music fitting their keen love.

And it joined them in singing
and dancing, and my Lady kept a fixed eye     110
on them just like a bride, quiet and still.

"This is he who lay upon Our
Pelican's breast; it is he who was asked
from the Cross, to assume the great office."

Thus my Lady. But her gaze                                          115
never lifted from its attending, nor were
words said either before or after.

Just as a person who squints
at eclipses, and tries to stare directly
becomes blinded by the light, so                                    120

did I at the last flame, until I heard
it say, "Why do you dazzle your senses
to see what has no place here?

On earth my body is earth,
and it lies there with the others until                             125
the Eternal tallies up the final number.

Two lights only in double garments
have risen to the blessed cloister. Tell
this to your world when you go back."

At this voice, the whirling flames                                  130
quieted, and with it the sweet mingling
of triune breath that had made their song,

just as when heavy oars, grown
risky as they toil through water, halt
together at the sound of a whistle.                                 135

Ah, how my mind was in commotion
when, turning to find Beatrice, I found instead
I could not see, though I was so close to her

and there we were in Paradise!

18. the Baron who draws souls to Galicia—St. James, who is buried in Galicia.

29–30. Renowned life, by whom the largesse of our church has been described—The Epistle of St. James.

33. his three—i.e., Peter, James, and John.

38. the second flame—St. James.

49. that pious one—i.e., Beatrice.

56. from Egypt to see Jerusalem—i.e., from slavery to the City of God.

82. It sighed—i.e., the soul of James.

84. the field of battle—i.e., earthly life.

94. your brother—St. John the Evangelist, who in Revelation 7:9 writes of multitudes standing before the Lamb in white robes, signifying the Elect.

98. *Sperent in te!*—Trust in you!

100. And then one soul—that of St. John.

112. This is he—i.e., John.

112–113. who lay upon Our Pelican's breast—John 13:23. "Now one of his disciples, he whom Jesus loved, was reclining upon Jesus' bosom"). The pelican was a traditional symbol for Christ. Medieval tradition held that pelicans fed their young with the blood of their breasts, which they would pierce with their beaks. Another tradition held that pelicans could revive their young from death with their blood.

113. he who was asked from the Cross, to assume the great office—John was asked to assume the care of Mary.

121. the last flame—John.

127. Two lights only—Jesus and Mary.

# Canto XXVI

[John and Dante discuss love, its source and power. At the conclusion
Dante's sight is restored. Dante then speaks with Adam, who tells him about
the garden of Eden.]


Standing there, shaken by the dazzling
flame that blinded me, there came a breath
that got my attention when it spoke, saying

"Until you have regained the sight
which your eyes consumed in me, it is                                    5
best that we compensate by talking.

So begin; say what the aim is
where you set your soul; but be assured
that your eyesight is only dazzled, not ruined.

The woman who conducts you                                              10
through these spheres has in a glance
the power that once lay in Ananias' hands."

I said, "As it pleases her, whether
sooner or later to cure the eyes that were
gates to the fire at which I always burn.                               15

The Good that contents this court
is the Alpha and Omega of all writing
that love reads to me, loud or soft."

The same voice that had soothed
my fear when I suddenly realized I could                                20
no longer see prompted me to speak again.

He said, "Of course you must sift
with a finer sieve. You must say what caused
you to draw your bow to such a mark."

And I: "By philosophical arguments                    25
and by authority descended from on high,
such love must imprint itself in me

    because the good, understood as such,
stirs into being more love, and the brighter
it is, the more we can see the good.                   30

    Thus in the essence is such
advantage that every other good is nothing
of itself but merely a ray of its light.

    So the mind of anyone capable
of seeing the truth beneath must be                    35
moved to love, more than anything.

    The truth of this is made plain
to my mind by him who reveals to me
the first love of every everlasting entity.

    As plain as it was made to Moses                   40
by the True Author, who said of Himself,
'I will show you a vision of true worth.'

    Made plain also in your high Gospel
which declaims its mysteries loudly from heaven
to earth, outstripping every other call."             45

    And I heard, "By human intellect
and by the authority in concordance with it,
the highest of your loves is love of God.

    But even if you feel other cords
pulling you to Him, you may declare                    50
how many teeth make up love's bite."

    The sacred purpose of Christ's
Eagle was not hidden; I knew how He
would want me to make my profession.

So I began again: "All those teeth                    55
with force to turn the heart to God
have been my charity all along.

The being of the world and my being,
the death he endured so that I might live,
the hope of all the faithful and of my own,          60

along with all I mentioned before,
drew me from the ocean of false love
and put me down on the shore of the true.

I love the leaves exfoliating
in the garden to the degree that each                65
has received the Eternal Gardener's ray."

As soon as I fell silent, a sweet song
resounded through heaven and My Lady
chanted with the others, "Holy! holy! holy!"

As a sharp light will jolt us awake                  70
because the visual spirit is in haste to meet
the splendor that goes from lid to lid

penetrating each of the eye's layers,
and the roused one abhors what he sees,
until judgment comes to the aid of sight,            75

so did Beatrice dispel every fleck
from my eyes with a look, whose brilliance
shot forth for over a thousand miles.

So I saw more keenly than ever
before and, all but stupefied, I asked               80
about a fourth light I saw in our midst.

And my Lady, "With those rays
there gazes the first work of its Maker,
the first soul that virtue ever created.

As a treetop bends in the course                    85
of the wind, then rights itself by means
of its own natural resilience,

so I bent in amazement while
he spoke, but regained my composure
and burning again with a desire to speak,          90

I began, "O first apple, alone
created ripe, O ancient father, to whom
all wives are daughters and daughters-in-law,

devotedly as I can, I beg you:
speak to me. You see my wish.                       95
I say less, that you may speak sooner."

Sometimes an animal will quiver
beneath a covering and so give away
its affect as it moves within.

So that primeval soul motioned                     100
its bliss through a transparent covering
and showed he joyed to bring me joy.

Then he breathed, "Though you
do not express your wish, I can discern it
more surely than what you hold most certain.       105

For I behold it in the True Mirror,
which is the faithful reflector of all things,
even though nothing can perfectly reflect It.

You want to know how long God
placed me in the high garden, where this Lady      110
prepared such a long ladder for you,

and how it brought pleasure
to my eyes, and the cause of the great
disdain, the language I made and used.

My son, it was not the tasting                           115
of the tree that was cause for so great exile,
but only the transgression of bounds.

Four thousand, three hundred, and two
suns I wished for this council from the place
where your Lady summoned Virgil.                         120

I saw the sun come around to all
the lights of this track nine hundred and thirty
times, while I lived on earth as man.

The language I spoke was already
extinct before Nimrod's gang were employed              125
to undertake their impossible task.

No product of reason can last
forever for man tends toward the stars
and changes as the stars change.

That man should speak is natural,                        130
but nature lets you decide, using this language
or that, how you wish to express yourself.

Until I was sent down to infernal
pain, I was called the Highest Good on earth,
and he wrapped me in all there was of joy;              135

then he was called El, as is proper,
because mortals' use is like leaves on a branch,
changing as they fall and are replaced.

I was on that mountain highest
from the sea, my life, first in innocence, then          140
disgrace, was from the first hour until the next,

the sixth, as the sun shifts quadrant."

## Notes

2. there came a breath—St. John.

12. Ananias—Ananias, by the laying on of hands, cured St. Paul's blindness (Acts ix).

38. him who reveals—The reference is to Aristotle.

51–52. Christ's Eagle—St. John.

83. the first soul—Adam.

124. Nimrod's gang—All people spoke an original language before the Tower of Babel.

135. El—According to St. Isadore's *Etymologie*, "El was the first name of God for the Hebrews." The other is Jehovah.

# Canto XXVII

[Peter denounces Boniface VIII for corruption and inveighs against church corruption generally. Dante and Beatrice make the ascent to the Primum Mobile, and she explains the movement and effect of this eighth sphere. Beatrice then turns to a discussion of the consequences of living in time.]

"Glory to the Father, to the Son,
and to the Holy Ghost!" began the sweet song
throughout Paradise, and I grew drunk with the sound.

What I seemed to see was the universe
turned into a smile, and thus my inebriation came          5
about through my hearing and seeing.

O joy!  O ineffable elation!
O perfect life of love and peace!
O secure wealth, wanting nothing more!

Before my eyes, the four torches                          10
were ablaze, and the one that first came
to me began to make itself brighter.

It appeared as Jove would have,
if he and Mars had been birds
who could exchange their feathers.                        15

That providence that distributes
the periods and services of each now imposed
silence on every side of the blessed choir.

When I heard, "Do not marvel
that I change color as I speak,                           20
for all these others change colors too.

He who usurps my place on earth,
my place, my place, my place, which now
before the Son of God stands vacant

has made my cemetery a sewer                    25
of blood and stench at which the Apostate
who fell from here is contented there."

Then I saw clouds painted the color
of dawn and evening, when they face sunward—
the same color I saw spread through heaven.       30

Just as a modest woman, secure
in herself, will blush for shame while
only listening to another's failings;

so did Beatrice's face change,
and I think this eclipse was the same one seen    35
in heaven when the Almighty suffered for us.

Then his words came forth in a voice
so transformed from its former self that
the look of him was not more changed.

"The Bride of Christ was not raised               40
on my blood, of Linus and of Cletus,
only to be used to grab gold;

it was for the gain of this joyous life
that Sixtus, Pius, Calixtus, and Urban,
after much wailing, shed their blood.             45

It was never our intention that our
successors, as Christian people, should sit,
part on the right hand, part on the left;

nor that the keys entrusted
to me become battle-flag symbols                  50
in a war waged against the baptized;

nor my profile to become a seal
endorsing dishonest and corrupt ends,
for which I often burn and blush.

It is clear the pastures are overrun                55
with voracious wolves in shepherd's garb:
o Godly defender, why do you sleep?

The Cahors and Gascons are
preparing to drink our blood: oh, how good
beginnings will in the end turn vile!               60

But high Providence that, with Scipio,
saved the glory of the world for Rome, will
again bring aid straightaway, I know.

You, my son, who must return
to mortal weight on earth, open your mouth:         65
do not hide what I do not hide from you.

As frozen vapors sift down
into our atmosphere when the horn
of the heavenly Goat touches the sun

so I saw the ether graced                           70
with rising mists, flying triumphantly,
which had once sojourned with us there.

My vision was tracking their images
until the medium by its very nature became
such that I couldn't follow them anymore.           75

The Lady who saw me freed
from looking upward said to me, " Look
down and see how far you have turned."

From the last time I had looked
I saw I had traversed the whole arc                 80
from the middle to the first climate.

There I saw the mad route
of Ulysses, and this side nearly to the shore
where Europa became a sweet cargo.

    I would have seen more of this                    85
threshing floor, except that I sensed
sun's motion beneath, a sign and beyond.

    My mind in love, so drawn
to My Lady, now more than ever
burned to look into her eyes.                          90

    And all that art or nature has made
to capture the eyes and so possess
the mind, whether in flesh or pictures,

    would appear as nothing compared
to the Divine delight that shone on me                 95
when I turned to her smiling face.

    That look endowed me with such
power I felt plucked from Leda's sweet nest
and propelled into swiftest heaven.

    Its parts are so swift and high,                   100
so uniform, that I cannot say where
Beatrice had chosen for my place.

    But she, who saw my desire,
began and smiled so joyously that it seemed
God rejoiced in her countenance.                       105

    "The nature of the world, whose
center is quiet, spins all the rest around it,
and so this heaven is the starting point.

    And there is no Where to this heaven
but the Mind of God, and the love that burns           110
turning it, and the power it rains.

    It is embraced by a circle of light
and love, surrounding and enclosing, and only
He who does the enclosing comprehends.

Its motion is not measured by another                       115
source: rather, it is the measure for all
the others, as ten is by half and fifth.

You can see how time's roots
are hidden in this sphere's vessel,
and how its leaves spread in the others.                     120

O greed that drags us down
to such a depth that no one can lift
his head to see above your waves!

The will blossoms well in men,
but the never-ending rain turns plums                        125
from ripe fruit into rotten skins.

For faith and innocence are found
only in children, then each flies off
before the cheeks have sprouted hair.

And one, still lisping, will observe                         130
fasts, but when his tongue is loosed, he gorges
on any food under whatever moon there is.

And one, still listing, will love
and mind his mother, but soon in mature
language will wish to see her buried.                        135

Thus white skin of that daughter
who brings us morning and leaves the night
turns black in the sight of Heaven.

Why wonder at what I say
when no one governs on earth                                 140
and so the human family goes astray.

Before January is unwintered,
owing to that day every hundred years
which men neglect, these spheres shall roar

with harbingers of the season's turning                    145
and sterns and prows of ships will change
places so that the fleet shall run its course

straight, and the true fruit follow the flower."

*Notes*

10. the four torches—Peter, John, Adam and James.

11. the one that first came—i.e., Peter.

22. He who usurps my place—Boniface VIII (c. 1230–1303). Dante placed
him in the Eighth Circle in the Inferno among the simoniacs (those who
offered money for spiritual authority).

26–27. the Apostate who fell—Satan.

41. Linus—traditionally held to be the Papal successor to Peter.

41. Cletus—successor to Linus.

44. Sixtus, Pius, Calixtus, and Urban—early Popes.

58. Cahors and Gascons—Clement V (1264–1314) from Gascony and John
XII from Cahors (1244–1334), both corrupt (i.e., French) Popes.

61. Scipio—Scipio's defeat of Hannibal is seen as providential, as it saved
Rome for the coming of Christianity.

69. the heavenly Goat—Capricorn.

82–83. the mad route of Ulysses—i.e., the Atlantic (see *Inferno*, XXVI).

84. where Europa became a sweet cargo—Zeus appeared to Europa as a bull
and carried her to Cadiz on his back.

86. threshing floor—i.e. the earth.

98. plucked from Leda's sweet nest—The union of Zeus (as a swan) and Leda
and in the same night her union with husband Tyndareus yielded the twins
Castor and Pollux, whom Zeus translated into the constellation Gemini.

# Canto XXVIII

[Dante looks back and witnesses the turning of the spheres and is astonished to see so many lights (angels). Beatrice explains the hierarchy of angels.]

After the Lady who put my mind
in Paradise had done exposing the miseries
that mortals encounter in this life,

like one who spies a candle
in a mirror and sees the glow before        5
he has a chance to see it whole

and turns round from the glass
to see in truth and finds it matches
the reflection, as notes do to music,

just so my memory recalls        10
after peering into those beautiful eyes,
in which Love set his snare,

and as I turned around, my eyes
were struck by what appeared there,
as when a man gazes deep into the gyre.        15

I saw a point of light shining
so piercingly that the face in which it
blazes would have to shut its eyes,

The star seen from here,
that seems smallest set beside this,        20
would, star to star, seem a moon.

Perhaps at the distance
that a halo is colored by a star
when vapors most often convey it,

so around the point a circle                                            25
of fire spun so rapidly it outsped
the motion of even the fastest sphere.

    Another one surrounded this,
the second by a third, the third by a fourth,
fourth by a fifth, the fifth by a sixth;                                30

    a seventh followed, so wide
now that Juno's messenger could not
contain it from one side to the other.

    So an eighth and ninth, each
revolving more slowly than the last, as                                 35
the number grew farther from the first.

    That one had most brightness
which was least distant, but which was also,
I believe, imbued with the greatest truth.

    My lady, who saw me perplexed                    40
and anxious said, "On that point
hang heaven and all of nature.

    Behold that circle nearest it
and understand that its spinning is so swift
because burning love sets it in motion."                                45

    And I: "If the world were ordered
as I perceive those wheels are, I would be
satisfied with what you have set before me;

    but in the world of the senses
it appears the turning spheres are the more                             50
divine the farther they are from the center.

    So if my desire is to find its end
in this miraculous and angelic temple,
where the only borders are love and light,

I still need to hear how the copy                           55
and the original are at odds because
when I contemplate this, I do so in vain."

"No need to wonder that your fingers
are incapable of loosening the knot;
not having been tried, it has tightened,"      60

my Lady said, then added: "If you
would be satisfied, then listen to what
I say and set your mind at its sharpest.

The physical spheres are wide
and narrow according to the virtue, more       65
or less, that expands through all their parts.

More goodness makes more well-being;
more well-being wants a bigger body, when
the body's parts are equally perfect.

Therefore this sphere, which sweeps            70
the rest of the universe before it, must correspond
to the circle that most loves and knows.

And so, if you take the measure
of the inherent virtue, not by way of substance,
which appears as roundness to you,             75

you will observe the admirable
result of greater to more and lesser to smaller
between each heaven and its Intelligence."

Just as the hemisphere of air
remains splendid and serene when it            80
blows from Boreas' gentler cheek,

the air becoming purified, dissolving
the mist that had veiled the sky, so heaven
laughs with the beauty of its pageantry,

as did I, when my Lady 85
made her lucid reply, and the truth
was seen like a star in heaven.

And when her speech was over,
no differently does molten iron give off
sparks than those circles also sparkled, 90

their coruscations all glitter, and so
many were there, that their number made
more millions than a chessboard doubled.

I heard their hosannas choir by choir
sung to the fixed point which has and always 95
shall hold them to the place where they

will forever be. And she who saw
my wonder, said, "The first circles
have shown you Seraphim and Cherubim.

They spin so following their bonds 100
to be as much like the point as they can,
and do so, as much as their vision is high.

Those other Loves circling them
are called Thrones of the Divine Aspect,
because they conclude the primal Triad. 105

And you should know that they
live in bliss as their vision fathoms
the Truth in which all intellect finds rest.

From this it may be seen
that blessedness lies with what one sees, 110
not in what one loves, which follows next.

The standard of vision is worth:
His grace brings it forward, as does their
good will: so it goes from grade to grade.

The second Triad, germinating                    115
in this eternal spring, that night,
under Ares, does not despoil,

warbles perpetual Hosannas
with threefold melody, whose sounds
suffuse the three orders of joy.                  120

In this hierarchy are the other
divinities: first Dominions, then Virtues,
and third in order, the Powers.

Then in the penultimate two,
Principalities and Archangels turn,               125
the last of all angelic celebration.

All these orders gaze upward,
while they also prevail downward, so that
all draw and all are drawn to God.

Dionysius, keen to contemplate                    130
these orders, set himself the task
of naming and ranking them, as I do.

Gregory, afterward, dissented,
but as soon as he opened his eyes in this
heaven, he had to smile at himself.               135

And if a mortal on earth revealed
such secrets, do not marvel, for the one
who saw it here revealed it to him

with many more truths about these rings."

*Notes*

32. Juno's messenger—Iris, the rainbow.

78. Intelligence—Each sphere has an angel, its "intelligence."

81. Boreas—the north wind. His "gentler cheek" would be the eastern or left cheek.

93. more millions than a chessboard doubled—When the inventor of chess, according to legend, showed his game to the king, the king was so pleased he asked what the inventor wanted as reward. He asked him to put a grain of wheat in the first square and then to double the amount of each successive square. To the king's astonishment, the final result was 18,000,000,000,000,000,000 grains. Dante doubles this amount to indicate the number of angels.

105. the primal Triad—Beatrice places the angelic orders in three Triads, or orders.

130. Dionysius—Dionysus the Areopagite, converted by Paul in Acts xvii. Dionysus wrote an exposition of the celestial hierarchy, *De Coelesti Hierarchia*.

133. Gregory—Gregory the Great ca. 540–604), Pope. He wrote of the celestial hierarchy, but Dante has him bemused by his harmless inaccuracies once he is in Heaven.

# Canto XXIX

[Beatrice's face is fixed on God as she explains creation and God's eternity. She then explains angelic time, before turning to a denunciation of false teachings.]

When both Latona's children
sit on the horizon line, the one rising
in Ares, the other setting in Libra,

as long as the zenith fulcrum
holds the scales in balance, until each                    5
moves, changing hemispheres,

just so long did Beatrice pause
smiling, her eye fixed on the Point
whose light I could not endure.

Then she began, "I do not ask;                             10
I say what you wish to hear, for I already
foresaw it where when and where are one.

It is not to acquire more good—
which is impossible—but because
reflected splendor may declare, I am,                      15

in His eternity outside time,
beyond all limits, as it pleased Him,
Eternal Love into new loves.

Nor was He idle before this;
for neither before nor after was, before                   20
God's going forth upon the waters.

Form and matter, joined or mixed,
came into being flawlessly like three
arrows shot from a three-stringed bow.

As in a glass, in amber or crystal,                    25
a sunbeam flashes so that no interval
exists between its coming and being,

just so the Sire's threefold effect:
his beam flashes, with no distinction, no
interval, into existence at once.                        30

Order was created in the substance
of things, and it was at the top of the world
where these ones were produced by pure act.

The lowest part held pure potential,
the middle tied potential with act,                      35
a bond that shall never be undone.

Hieronymo wrote you about the stretch
of centuries between the making of angels
and the creation of the rest of the world,

but such is written in many places                       40
by writers inspired by the Holy Spirit,
and you will find it if you read carefully.

Even reason can grasp it partially:
it cannot concede that angelic powers
could exist so long minus perfection.                    45

But now you know where and when
and how these Loves came to be, thus
quenching three flames of your desire.

But faster than you could count
to twenty, a party of these angels                       50
shook the elemental foundations.

The rest remained and began
the dance that you see here with such delight
that their whirling goes on forever.

The reason for the Fall lay          55
in the presumption of one you saw below
crushed by the weight of the world.

These others you see humbly
acknowledged the goodness that made
them capable of great understanding,       60

so that their vision was raised
to such a degree by God's enlightening grace
that their will is committed and whole.

Now beyond a doubt it is certain
that this grace is received in proportion     65
as the heart is open to receive it.

And now, if you have taken
my word, you should be able to consider
this sacred body without further aid.

But since on earth you teach         70
in school that the angelic nature includes
understanding, memory and will,

I will say more, because you see
the pure truth here that is confounded
below by ambiguous teachings.       75

Since they first saw it, these beings
took delight in the face of God, for whom nothing
is hidden, and they never turned away.

As a result, their sight is never
divided by something new; they have     80
therefore no need for memory.

So on earth men dream awake
believing or not the truth of what they say
and in the end, more's the sin and shame.

Your philosophizing does not                    85
lead you down a path to certainty: rather,
you find infatuation in appearance and wit.

Yet even this is met here above
with less insult than when the Holy Writ
is greeted with disregard or traduced.          90

Men do not seem to care how much
blood is required to plant it in the world,
nor how pleasing is the humble, devoted man.

Each is pretentious, a master
of inventions, which preachers pass on as if     95
gospel, while the real Gospel is silent.

This one says the moon went
backwards to eclipse the sun during the Passion
so that it was deprived of light—he lies.

That light hid itself, and hence                 100
Spaniards and Indians alike, responded
to the same eclipse as the Jews.

Such fables are shouted
from the pulpits left and right, more
in a year than are Lapi and Bindi in Florence!   105

So that the sheep, knowing no
better, come from pasture full of wind:
their blindness from harm being no excuse.

Christ did not say to the disciples,
'Go into the the world and preach nonsense'      110
but rather gave them a foundation of truth.

With only this on their lips they
went forth fighting to kindle their faith,
having only the Gospel for lance and shield.

Now men go forth to preach jokes,                    115
anything to make the people laugh,
to puff up their hoods: that's all they want.

But in the cowl is such a bird
that if the people were to see, they would
know the kind of pardons they had relied on.        120

So much folly has grown on earth
that, without testimonial proof, they run
after whatever promise is offered them.

By this is St. Anthony's pig made fat,
and others, who are worse than swine,               125
pay their way with counterfeit money.

But we have digressed. Therefore,
turn your eyes back to the true path
so as to adjust our time to the journey.

This nature multiplies itself in such               130
grand numbers that there is no speech
that can keep up, nor human fancy.

If you look at what is said
in the Book of Daniel, you will see that
in his thousands the actual number is hidden.       135

The First Light shines and irradiates
them all in as many ways as there
are splendors for it to penetrate.

Thus, since the visual act precedes
the act of love, the sweetness within varies        140
accordingly, whether burning or warming.

And now you see the pinnacle
and breadth of Eternal Worth, seeing
itself divided and mirrored, reflecting Itself

as One, as it was before."                          145

## Notes

1. both Latona's children—Apollo, the sun, and Diana, the moon.

37. Hieronymo—i.e., St. Jerome (ca. 342–420), one of the most learned of the Church Fathers.

105. Lapi and Bindi—common Florentine names.

118. But in the cowl is such a bird—i.e., Satan.

124. St. Anthony's pig—St. Anthony the Great (ca. 251–356) was commonly depicted with a pig, representing the demons with whom he would have struggled in the desert. Here, it represents corrupt clergy.

# Canto XXX

[Dante and Beatrice ascend to the Empyrean, where he sees her true beauty. He sees a reflection of the Mystic Rose composed of heavenly beings, ranked tier on tier. Beatrice ends her discourse by prophesying against Vatican sins, then returns to silence.]

About six thousand miles away,
high noon burns, while here the earth's shadow
slants to an almost level bed;

thus at the zenith, the deep sky
begins to change so that some stars                    5
begin to fade from our sight.

And as the sun's brightest handmaid
approaches, and the heavens begin to close,
light by light, until even the prettiest fades,

just so the Triumph that perpetually                   10
plays around the Point that overpowered me,
that seems enclosed by what it encloses,

faded little by little from my sight.
And thus, seeing nothing more, love
constrained me to turn my eyes to Beatrice.            15

If everything that has been said
of her were reduced to a single phrase
it would be of scant service to me now.

The beauty I beheld transcends
not only our mortal grasp, but truly I                 20
believe only its Creator can appreciate it.

From this point I admit myself beat:
never was there a comic or a tragic poet
who was so undone by his theme.

For as the sun does to the eyes                                       25
so does the memory of that sweet smile
dash the sense from my mind.

The first day I saw her face
in this life, up to this present sight: such
has been the armature of my song.                                    30

But now I must put by such
pursuit, for I have done as much as any
artist can do to track eternal beauty.

So I leave her to a greater fame
than proclaimed by my trumpet,                                       35
as the difficult ending draws near

and she, with the voice and manner
of a guide began, "We have gone on from
the greatest sphere to the heaven of pure light:

intellectual light, filled with love,                                40
love of good compounded with joy,
joy that transcends every sweetness.

Here you will see one and the other
legion of paradise, and one in the same aspect
as you will see it at the Final Judgment."                           45

Just as sudden lightning scatters
the spirits of sight and in so doing deprives
the eye of even the clearest object,

so too the living light flashed
around me and left me enclosed in such                               50
a veil of brightness that I could see nothing.

"The love that calms the sky
always welcomes with such salutation
as the candle is readied for the flame."

No sooner had these words                                    55
made their way into me than I became
aware of much-heightened powers;

    such new vision lit my sight
that even the brightest beam was not
too bright, so fortified were my eyes.                       60

    I saw the light as a river
that blazed in sparks on either bank
painted with colors of spring.

    From this river living sparks
flew up and then sank on flowers                             65
that looked like rubies set in golden rings.

    As if inebriated by the odors
they plunged into the miraculous stream,
and as one dove in, another flew up.

    "The high desire that inflames               70
and impels you on to seek understanding
pleases me more as it burns more.

    But first you must drink of the waters,
if you are to slake so great a thirst."
So said the sunshine of my eyes.                             75

    She added, "The river and the topazes
that come and go, the laughter of the grass:
these are prefaces prefiguring their truth.

    This is not to say they are imperfect;
rather, the flaw lies in your seeing, which                 80
is not yet ready to attain such heights."

    There is no infant, having slept
too long, who jolts awake and turns his face
to the milk, who was more eager than I

as I stooped to the stream 85
that flows for our improvement,
to make keener mirrors of the eyes.

But even as the eaves of my eyes
drank, I thought I saw the river change
course from straight to round. 90

Then, as masqueraders divest
themselves of the masks and show
true selves instead of semblances

just so the flowers and sparks
changed into something grander, and I 95
saw both courts of Heaven made manifest.

O splendor of God, through which
I beheld the high triumph of the true realm!
Grant me the power to say what I saw!

There is a light above that makes 100
the Creator's face visible to every creature,
whose only peace lies in the beholding.

The shape of the light as it ripples
outward is circular, its circumference
would out-girdle the sun. 105

All of that radiance originates
from a light reflected off the top of the Primum
Mobile, which derives life and power from it.

And as a water-circled hillside
is reflected at the base, almost as if to 110
let it see its own greenery and flowers,

so, mirrored, I saw in more than
a thousand echelons how many of us
there were here who had won return.

And if the lowest rank can bear                    115
so great a light, how vast the fullness
of this Rose to its farthest petals!

In all the reach and height my eyes
comprehended what they saw, both
in the quantity and quality of that joy.          120

There neither near nor far
has meaning, for where God governs
directly natural law has no relevance.

Into the yellow of the Eternal Rose
that spreads its petals arises the fragrance       125
of praise for the sun of perpetual spring,

Beatrice drew me, in silence,
though I wanted to speak, and said, "Look
at how vast the assembly of white robes is!

See our city, how it sprawls;                      130
see how our seats are so filled that
there is scant room left for more!

In that seat that draws your eyes
where a crown already waits above it,
shall sit, before you sit down to this wedding     135

feast, the soul of the great Henry,
future Emperor, who will one day come
to straighten Italy before she is ready.

Blind greed has cast its spell
on you like a child who is starving                140
and yet pushes his nurse away.

The prefect of the sacred court
will be one who will walk with him openly
but work against him in secret.

But God will not suffer him long                145
in holy office: he shall be thrust down
where Simon Magus serves his sentence

and he shall force him, Alagna, deeper down."

*Notes*

136–137. soul of the great Henry, future Emperor—Henry VII, count of
Luxembourg (1275–1313). Shortly after his coronation in 1305, he announced
his intention to travel to Florence, where he intended to secure the fealty of the
Ghibellines and to unite the warring Italian factions (and, Dante hoped, to
bring about his return from exile). Traveling on to Rome, he contracted a
disease, probably malaria, and died without succeeding in his political aim.
142. prefect of the sacred court—The prefect is the Pope; the sacred court, the
Vatican. Dante intends Clement V (1264–1314) who deceived Henry into
believing he supported him.
146. Simon Magus—the religious leader whose conflict with Peter is recorded
in Acts viii. The sin to which he lent his name—the commercial traffic in
churchly prerogatives, (e.g., pardons) lands him in the *Inferno* (XIX).
147. Alagna—Boniface VIII (ca. 1230–1303), born Alagna. Although Boniface
was still alive as of the writing of the *Commedia*, Dante places his soul in Hell
(*Inferno* XIX), among the simoniacs, each of whom is jammed head down in a
parody of the baptismal font. Newcomers force the sufferers to be buried
vertically even deeper. These are Beatrice's last words in the *Commedia*.

# Canto XXXI

[Dante encounters St. Bernard of Clarivaux, who will be his final guide, as
Beatrice takes her throne in the Rose. Dante says a farewell prayer of thanks to
Beatrice, who smiles at him a final time, before turning to God. St. Bernard
tells Dante to look up.]

In the shape of a white Rose,
the sacred host was shown me that Christ,
in His own blood, had made His Bride.

The other host—flying and singing
the glory of Him that drew them to His love          5
and the goodness that so ennobled it,

like a swarm of bees that in one moment
dive into the flowers and in another turn
back to the sweet work of the hive—

plunged into the great, man-                          10
petaled bloom, and then flew back
to the place where eternal love reposes.

Their faces were living flame,
and their wings were gold, the rest so
white no snow could rival it.                         15

As they entered the flower,
they spread, level by level, both ardor
and peace by the fanning of their flanks.

Nor did such plenty interposed
between the flower and what was above                 20
impede the sight and splendor.

The Divine Light so thoroughly
pervades the universe according to the merit
of each part that nothing can stop it.

This secure and happy realm                               25
was thronged with old and new, who trained
their look and love all to one end.

O Triple Light, that sparkles
in their eyes, contenting from a single light,
look down upon us in our storm!                           30

If the barbarians (who come
from that place where Helice travels the sky
with her beloved son each day)

seeing Rome and her mighty works
were dumbfounded (when the Lateran               35
outshone all mortal achievements)

then imagine, when I came
from human to the divine, time to eternity,
from Florence to the just and sane,

the size of my utter stupor!                                   40
Truly between this and my new joy
it was a pleasure neither to hear nor speak.

As a pilgrim at the shrine of his vow
is renewed and considers, as he looks around,
how to describe it when he returns home,          45

so did I survey the living light,
leading my eyes through the degrees,
now up, now down, now sweeping about.

There I saw faces devoted to love
of His light and by smiles and demeanor           50
embellished with every grace.

At this point my vision had grasped
the general plan of Paradise but had not
focused on any particular part,

and with renewed desire to know                    55
I turned around to ask my Lady about
things of which I was still unsure.

What I expected was not what I met:
I thought I would see Beatrice but saw instead
an elder dressed in the robes of the blessed.         60

His eyes and cheeks were flushed
with divine joy, and he had a tender
father's bearing of compassion.

I said at once, "Where is she?"
He replied, "She urged me to leave my place           65
and come to bring an end to your longing.

If you look up to the third circle,
highest degree, you will see her enthroned
where merit ordained she should be."

Without reply I raised my eyes                        70
and saw that she had made herself
a crown that reflected the eternal light.

Not from the region of highest
thunders, to the bottom of the deepest sea
was any eye so far as mine then                       75

was from Beatrice, but it
made no difference because her image
came to me without any blur.

"O Lady, in whom resides my hope,
and who for my salvation was suffered                 80
to leave the imprint of her feet in hell,

it is thanks to your excellence
and power that I have recognized virtue
and grace in all the things I have seen.

You led me, a slave, to freedom                    85
by all those ways and using all the means
that were within your power to employ.

Preserve me in your magnificence,
so that my soul, brought to health, may be
pleasing to you when it leaves the body."          90

So I entreated her, and she, so
distant as it seemed, looked down and smiled,
then turned back to the eternal fountain.

The holy elder said, "In order that your
journey may reach its perfect consummation         95
prayer and sacred love have sent me.

Let your eyes fly in this garden
for gazing at it will train your sight
to rise and follow along the divine ray.

The Queen of Heaven, in whose                      100
fires my love burns, will grant us every grace
because I am her faithful Bernard."

And like a foreigner, a Croatian
perhaps, who comes to gaze at our Veronica
and cannot get his fill of that ancient fame,      105

but says to himself while it is
displayed, "My Lord Christ, true God,
is this what you looked like in life?"

Just so I found that I was gazing
at the living love of one who in this world,       110
in contemplation, tasted of that peace.

He began, "Son of grace, you
will not know this state of blissful being
if you keep your eyes trained on what's below.

Instead, let your eyes rise to the most          115
distant circles, until they behold the Queen
to whom this realm is subject and devoted."

I raised my eyes, and as the morning
horizon in the east shines brighter
than where the sun sets, and I saw,          120

as if going with my eyes
from valley to mountaintop, a remote part
that shown more splendidly than all the rest.

And even as on earth we await
Phaeton's shaft at the brightest          125
point, while the sides grow dim,

just so there in the center
the golden standard of peace shown
and on each side the glow subsided,

while all about the center, I saw          130
the outstretched wings of a thousand euphoric
angels, each different in brightness and kind.

And I saw smiling there, at their festivity
and song, a beauty whose joy was reflected
in the eyes of all the other saints.          135

If I had as great riches in words
as in imagining, I would not dare attempt
even the smallest part of such delight.

When Bernard saw how my eyes
were fixed on the object of his zeal turned          140
his own eyes to her with such love that he

made my own gaze all the more intense.

## Notes

2. the sacred host—Dante is shown two hosts: those who were in heaven, having lived first on earth, and those whose entire existence had been heaven.

32. Helice—a nymph who bore a son to Zeus (Arcas). For this, Hera changed her into a bear and translated her to heaven (Ursa Major), along with her son (Ursa Minor).

35. the Lateran—The Lateran Palace was the papal residence during Dante's lifetime.

60. but saw instead an elder—St. Bernard of Clarivaux (1090–1153). Cistercian monk and reformer who helped to spread the Benedictine Order and devotee of Mary, known for his eloquence and contemplative nature. He is Dante's final guide.

104–105. a Croatian perhaps—i.e., as one on the margins of Christendom, although Croatians were known for the strength of their faith.

104. our Veronica—i.e., "true icon." The Veronica was a cloth used to wipe the sweat from Christ's face as he made his way to Calvary. It reputedly bore His image and was put on display and venerated in the Vatican.

125. Phaeton's shaft—i.e., the forwardmost part of Phaeton's chariot to be seen at dawn.

# Canto XXXII

[Bernard identifies the souls that make up the Mystic Rose. All the while, Bernard has kept his gaze on the vision of the Virgin Mary, and he invites Dante to join him in a prayer to her.]

Engrossed in what he most loved
that contemplative freely offered himself
as guide and began with these holy words:

"The wound that Mary closed
and healed was the wound that lovely one          5
who sits at her feet opened and pierced.

Below her, in the third order
Rachel sits, and lower from her,
there with Beatrice, as you can see,

are Sarah, Rebecca, Judith, and she               10
who was great granddaughter of the singer
who cried, '*Miserere mei!*,' for his sins.

You can clearly see as I descend
from station to station, petal to petal, down
the Rose, and I give each one its name.           15

From the seventh row down, as
with up, are the Hebrew women in succession,
parting all the petals of the Rose.

Because according to the view
of Christ they held, they are the wall            20
dividing the ranks down the sacred stairs.

On one side, where the Rose
is in bloom down to every petal, sit those
who had faith in Christ yet to come,

and on the other, where the semicircles                25
are intersected by empty spaces, sit those
who turned to Christ already come.

And just as on this side
is the Lady of Heaven's throne, with
the lower seats forming the dividing wall,              30

so across, facing, is the throne
of the great John, who suffered the desert,
martyrdom, and two years in Hell;

and below him, forming the wall,
sit Francis, Benedict, and Augustine,                   35
as well as others, rank on rank to the center.

Now behold God's divine providence,
for this and that aspect of the faith shall
in equal measure fill the garden.

And know that as you go down                            40
from the center which cleaves the two divisions
no soul may claim a seat by merit,

but by another's, under certain conditions
because all these are souls who were absolved
of sin before they reached the age of free choice.     45

You can see it for yourself in their faces
and also in their young voices, if you
observe them well and listen to them.

But you doubt and do not speak.
So now I will loosen the knot                           50
that has entangled you in thought.

Inside the sweep of this domain
no point exists by chance, just as there
is no room for sadness, thirst, or hunger.

For Eternal Law has been ordained                    55
for everything that you see here: the ring
and the finger make a perfect fit.

Therefore, all these people
in the true life here are not ranked higher
or lower without sufficient cause.                    60

The King on whom this realm
reposes in so great a love and such joy
that no one would wish for greater,

creating every mind in His joyous
purview, granting grace at his pleasure;              65
let the fact itself be enough.

Holy Scripture records this
for you, concerning those twins who were
roused to anger in their mother's womb.

So it is fitting that the Light Supreme               70
confers its grace, to each his merit,
shown by the color of his hair.

Therefore, through no merit
of works, they are accorded rank differently,
the difference being God's grace.                     75

In early times, it was enough
for parents' faith to validate the innocence
of children and so secure their salvation.

Then when the first age of man
was complete, circumcision of males                   80
gave strength to innocent wings.

But then the age of grace came
and without the perfect baptism of Christ
innocence was confined, below, to Limbo.

Now look into the face that most                                   85
resembles Christ, for you may only see
Him if you have first clarified your eyes."

    I saw such a joy rain down,
carried by all those holy minds
created to soar to that height                                     90

    that whatever I had seen before
had not gripped my soul more than this, neither
did it show me such likenesses of God.

    That love that first descended
chanting, *Ave Maria, gratia plena*,                               95
now stood before her with wings spread.

    From every part of this blessed
court came a divine hymn in response
so that each face became more serene.

    "O Holy Father, who stands down                                100
here for my sake, leaving behind the sweet
throne in which you sit by eternal order,

    who is that angel who looks
with such bliss into the eyes of our Queen,
so full of love he seems aflame?"                                  105

    Thus I sought out the teaching
of him who drew his beauty from Mary,
as the morning star draws beauty from the sun.

    And he to me, "There is in him
such gallantry and grace as can be found                           110
in angel or soul, and so we would have it.

    For he was the one who bore
the palm down to Mary, when the Son of God
took upon himself our body as his own.

Now let your eyes follow my words                    115
as I talk and take note of the great patricians
of this just and pious empire.

Those two who sit most blissfully
for being near the Empress are,
so to speak, the taproots of this Rose.               120

The one who sits to the left
is the father, by whose foolhardy appetite
bitterness was bequeathed to humankind.

To the right see that ancient who
is the Father of our Holy Church, to whom            125
Christ gave the keys to this lovely flower.

And he who, before his death,
foresaw the troubles of the beautiful bride
won by nails and spear, sits to his right.

Beside the first man sits that leader                 130
under whom the people lived on manna:
ungrateful, fickle, and stubborn.

Facing Peter you see Anna seated,
perfectly content to gaze on her daughter,
her eyes unmoving as she sings Hosanna.               135

And opposite mankind's great father
sits Lucia, who first moved your Lady
to your aid, when you were brow-bent on ruin.

But because the moments of vision
fly by, I will stop here to make a point,             140
like the tailor who fits gown to cloth,

so turn your eyes toward Primal Love
and in gazing at Him, your sight may reach
as far as it can into His radiance.

But lest you should fall back                           145
thrashing wings as if you were moving
forward, you must ask for grace through prayer,

grace from the one who has the power,
so follow me, with devoutest love so that
your heart does not turn from my words."              150

And he began this sacred prayer.


*Notes*

5–6. that lovely one who sits at her feet opened and pierced—i.e., Eve.

8. Rachel—the younger wife of Jacob.

10. Sarah—wife of Abraham.

10. Rebecca—wife of Isaac.

10. Judith—She beguiles the Assyrian commander Holofernes and when he is asleep, she decapitates him. The Assyrian forces are subsequently routed and the Jews saved. (Book of Judith)

10–12. she was the great granddaughter … who cried… *'Miserere mei!,'* for his sins—The figure is Ruth, great granddaughter of King David. David lusted after the married Bathsheba and sent her husband to his death in battle (Psalm 51).

32. the great John—John the Baptist, who was beheaded two years before the crucifixion and was rescued by Christ, after two years in Limbo, in the Harrowing of Hell, and led to Heaven.

68. those twins—Jacob and Esau. In Genesis xxv, they are already in opposition in their mother's womb.

85–86. Now look into the face that most resembles Christ—i.e., Mary.

94–95. That love that first descended chanting, *Ave Maria, gratia plena*—the Archangel Gabriel, who delivered the Annunciation, "Hail Mary, full of grace!"

122. the father—Adam.

124. To the right see that ancient—St. Peter.

127–128. And he who, before his death, foresaw the troubles—St. John, who foretold the troubles of the Church in the Apocalypse.

130. that leader—Moses.

133. Anna—Mother of Mary.

137. Lucia—It was St. Lucia who sent Beatrice to rescue Dante.

# Canto XXXIII

[Bernard asks the Virgin to bless Dante, and he is given a vision of God. He declares himself incapable of describing the vision, except in its most modest, mortal, limited part, but he is heartened to realize that he partakes of that Love and that his soul will return.]

"Virgin Mother, daughter of your Son,
more humble and exalted than any creature,
established by eternal decree, you

    are the one who brought nobility
to human nature, so that even as its Creator      5
He did not disdain to make himself a man.

    Love was rekindled in your womb
so that this flower germinated in its warmth
to blossom into an eternal peace.

    To those here you are      10
the noonday torch of charity, and below
in the mortal world, the fountain of hope.

    Lady, so great and powerful,
that whoever wants grace without resort
to you would desire to fly with no wings.      15

    Your kindness gives comfort
to those who ask, but oftentimes
you give it freely before the asking.

    In you is mercy. In you, pity.
In you, magnificence. All that is good      20
in God's creatures unites in you.

    From the deepest pit of the universe
to as far as the eye can see, this man
has seen, one by one, the three lives.

He brings his supplication to you,                    25
that by your grace he may find the strength
to raise his eyes to the ultimate well-being.

And I, who never burned for my
own vision more than for his, give you all
of my prayers and pray they are adequate,             30

that you, with our own prayers
can banish the fog of his mortality so that
he may find the Final Happiness revealed.

I pray you, Queen, who can make
all your wishes real, to keep his affections          35
strong, after so extraordinary a vision.

May your protection overcome
flesh's ways: see how Beatrice and all the Blest,
with clasped hands, join my prayer."

The eyes loved and revered by God,                    40
fixed on the speaker, showed us how
cherished devout prayers are to her.

Then she turned her eyes
to the Eternal Light; it is not believable
that any other creature could see so clearly.         45

And I, who was near the end
of all desires, as I should have, felt myself
straining to raise my yearning aloft.

Bernard smiled to me and signaled
that I turn my eyes upward, but I knew                 50
already instinctively what he wished of me,

for as my sight became purified
it was more and more able to penetrate
the lofty light, which is truth itself.

From that moment on, what I saw                    55
was greater than speech, which must yield
to vision, and memory likewise must yield.

As a man who dreams and wakes
to find that passion's imprint remains
but the rest does not return to mind,               60

just such am I: for my vision
almost ceases completely, and still in my heart
there is distilled the sweetness born of it.

So snow is unsealed in the sun,
and so wind in the leaves blows                      65
the Sibyl's oracle and its judgment away.

O Supreme Light, so far beyond
the comprehension of mortals, return
something of your revelation to me

and give my tongue power                             70
to bequeath to future people a single
spark of your glory. For by restoring

something of my memory to mind
and by sounding—even a little—in my verses
more of your victory will be pictured.              75

I believe I would be lost
if I had averted my eyes to the living ray
and the searing brilliance they endured.

I remember that this emboldened me
to keep gazing into it so that my aspect            80
lined up with the Infinite Glory.

O grace abounding by which
I presumed to set my sight on the Eternal
Light, so that it was consumed!

In its depths I saw how it contained                        85
all, bound by love, in a single volume,
of which the world is scattered leaves.

Substances, accidents, and their
ways were interfused in such a manner
that my speaking of it was elementary.                      90

I believe I saw the universal form,
the intertwining of all things, since I
can feel a fuller joy in speaking this.

One moment brings me more
lethargy than twenty-five centuries that                    95
passed since Neptune saw Argus' keel.

So my mind was held in suspension,
steadfast, immobile, attentive, and I
burned the more the more I gazed.

In that light one becomes                                   100
so changed that it is almost impossible
to imagine turning away from it

because the good, the object
of the will, gathered all in this, and what is
outside it is defective, what is here—perfect.              105

Even what I remember has
no more force than an infant who wets
his tongue at the breast of his mother.

and not because the living light
on which I looked had more than one                         110
aspect, for it is always what it was.

But in the looking, my sight
became strengthened, and that one aspect
seemed to change as I changed.

Within its deep, luminous existence                    115
the High Light appeared as three rings
of three colors and a single dimension;

the one from the other, as rainbow
is from rainbow, second from first, and the third
seemed fire breathed equally from both.                120

Oh, how dimly my speech falls
compared to my conception, and yet
to call it "little" is to call it too much.

O Eternal Light fixed on Yourself,
and only known to Yourself, and Self-                  125
knowing, you love and smile upon Yourself!

The circling, as I saw it, appeared
in you as a reflected light, and when
I looked into it with contemplation

it seemed, both in itself and of                       130
the same color to be painted with our effigy.
My sight was all absorbed in it.

As the geometer tries to square
the circle, but cannot find, through
thought on thought, the key,                           135

I was like that with the new mystery.
I wished to understand how our image
suited the circle and yet found no place there,

but my wings were not sufficient;
then my mind was struck, and in a lightning            140
flash I was granted my wish.

At this point my high fantasy failed,
but now I could feel myself turning like a wheel,
and I felt my desire and will impelled by that

Love that moves the sun and the other stars.           150

*Note*

66. the Sibyl's oracle—In the *Aeneid*, the Sibyl composed her oracles on leaves. Thus, sorting the letters—the work of the poet—completes the prophecy.

# A Note on the Translation

It was my mentor Brodsky who first impressed upon me the importance of reading Dante—in translation. Brodsky had a theory that some poets do better in translation than in the original, although Dante was not one of these. Nonetheless, it was still incumbent on the translator to be as exacting as possible. It was only a skip from that conjecture to the idea that some others among these same poets intended to wind up in translation, presumably in order to sound removed, in exile, possibly posthumous. In any case, it certified alienation of a closer sort (one's language) to be more representative of the tone of oneself in a foreign language than in the original. Brodsky, I imagine, was keeping an eye on his own poems, destined (or cursed) to reappear in English. I once asked him, "How much should one try to keep? Rhyme? Meter? Puns?" I remember the force of his answer: "Everything!" No doubt he knew that his own poems occasionally, laden as they are with baroque poetic baggage, raised some eyebrows among the English-speaking readership, regardless of their being rendered by poets of undoubtable stature. Be that as it may, he implicitly expected Dante in English to include terza rima, the indispensable hendecasyllabic line, original wordplay, and word-for-word accuracy. In other words, he wanted the impossible. Dante puts the case for impossibility up front when he confesses that his goal is unattainable. How much beyond impossibility, then, for the translator of Dante? Clarence Brown, the Mandelstam translator remarked that no translation could do damage to the original. However, the fact that we can't know all languages opens the door not only to translation but to the obligation translators have to justify their versions of "carrying over," keeping in mind Borges' sly advisory about translations that "not a word in them is justified."

Italian takes from its Romantic linguistic roots the advantage that words rhyme easily (for example, so many end in vowels), but English, while it's good for the sturdiness and facility of Romance (or Slavic or classical) meters, falls short of delivering when it comes to rhyme. John Ciardi, perhaps most widely read among poet-translators of Dante, attempted something of the sound of the original, but he did so by omitting the middle (i.e., the A-B-A, B-C-B...) rhyme that, by reappearing in the next stanza as the outer rhymes, threads the narrative into a fabric. Even this much fealty to the original form drove Ciardi to feats of paraphrase and occasional posturing, leaving the literal in the dust. Robert Pinsky's celebrated and energetic version of the *Inferno* went for slant rhymes ("died/. . . vowed/. . . lewd"), but at the expense full rhyme's bell-tone attraction. Only Ciaran Carson, among contemporaries, has tried the rhyme scheme in his *Inferno* (setting aside Clive James' rhymed quatrains). Still, one searches for a way to render what one reviewer has called "the cadenced tautness" of the Italian. And it so happens that one of our premiere poet-translators, W. S. Merwin, has succeeded at just that in his translation of the *Purgatorio*. But then, Merwin has made a dual career of pursuing both the strengths and characteristics of English at its baseline in his own poems and of French, Italian, and Provençal verse in translation. His is writing-degree-zero, without unnecessary affect, and as a result, one begins to see—and hear—something like what plausibly it might have been to hear Dante's verse in 1321. It is a remarkable feat of linguistic humility too but customary for Merwin. I also have admiration for Mandelbaum's close, sturdy version of the *Paradiso*, and have kept it by my side, along with Ciardi's, Mark Musa's, and the ever-indispensable prose version of Charles Singleton, over the four-plus years this project took, but I have found the Merwin version most readable and therefore most exemplary. Although I have worked both in free verse and rhyme (and published a collection of sonnets, both Shakespearean and Italian), my bias has been to look to Merwin's example, trying to find that tautness, which has the authority and expressiveness of understatement, and is no less winged than its rhetorical obverse, toward which the heirs of the Elizabethans and our own formalists sharpened their quills.

# About the Author

David Rigsbee is the author of over twenty books and chapbooks, including twelve previous full-length collections of poems. In addition, he has published critical works on Carolyn Kizer and Joseph Brodsky, whom he also translated. He has co-edited two anthologies, including *Invited Guest: An Anthology of Twentieth Century Southern Poetry,* as well as a critical collection, *Not Alone in My Dancing: Essays and Reviews.* His work has appeared in *AGNI, The American Poetry Review, The Georgia Review, The Iowa Review, The New Yorker, Poetry, Prairie Schooner, The Sewanee Review, The Southern Review*, and many others. He has received a Pushcart Prize, two creative writing fellowships from the National Endowment for the Arts, and a NEH summer fellowship to the American Academy in Rome. His other awards include a Fine Arts Work Center in Provincetown fellowship, the Virginia Commission on the Arts literary fellowship, the Djerassi Foundation and Jentel Foundation residencies, and an Award from the Academy of American Poets. His *Watchman in the Knife Factory: New and Selected Poems* will be published in 2024. He lives in the Hudson Valley of New York.

# salmonpoetry

Cliffs of Moher, County Clare, Ireland

*"Publishing the finest Irish and international literature."*
Michael D. Higgins, President of Ireland